About Skill Builders Geometry

by Tiffany Moore

Welcome to RBP Books' Skill Builders series. Like our Summer Bridge Activities collection, the Skill Builders series is designed to make learning both fun and rewarding.

Skill Builders *Geometry* introduces students to beginning geometry concepts to help them reinforce and develop math skills. Each Skill Builders volume is grade-level appropriate, with clear examples and instructions to guide the lesson. In accordance with NCTM standards, exercises for Geometry cover a variety of math skills, including shapes, perimeter and area, circumference, congruence and symmetry, volume, and angles.

A critical thinking section includes exercises to develop higher-order thinking skills.

Learning is more effective when approached with an element of fun and enthusiasm. That's why the Skill Builders combine entertaining and academically sound exercises and fun themes to make reviewing basic skills fun and effective, for both you and your budding scholars.

www.summerbridgeactivities.com

Table of Contents

Matching—Shapes

Match the definition to the shape.

Example:

__H__ is a polygon with six sides.

1. ____ is a quadrilateral with opposite sides parallel.
2. ____ is a polygon with three angles.
3. ____ is an eight-sided polygon.
4. ____ is a plane figure with four equal sides and four right angles. Opposite sides are parallel.
5. ____ is a five-sided polygon.
6. ____ is an irregular polygon.
7. ____ is a quadrilateral with four right angles. Opposite sides are parallel, but not all sides are equal.
8. ____ is a quadrilateral with two sides not parallel and two sides parallel.

A 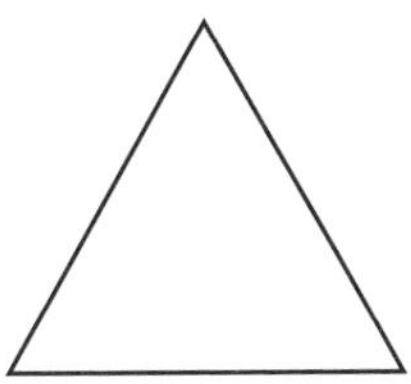

B 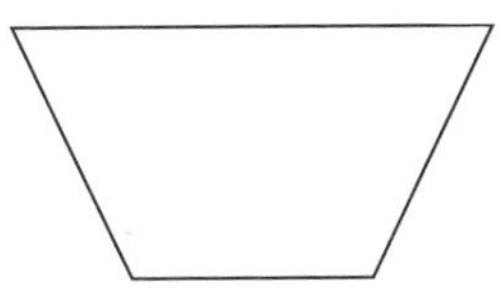

C 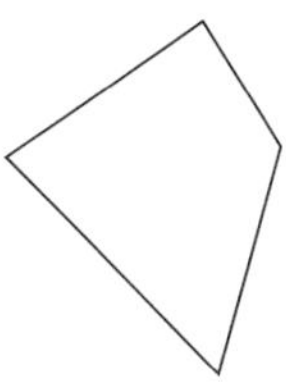

D 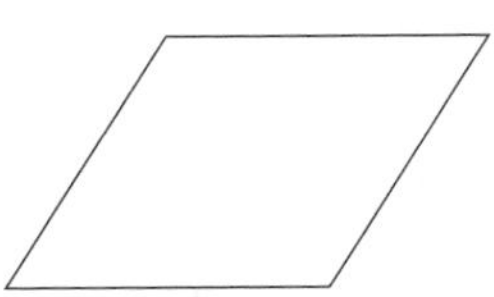

E 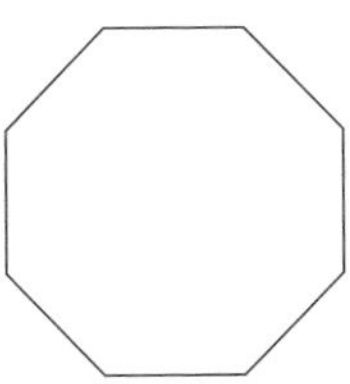

F 

G 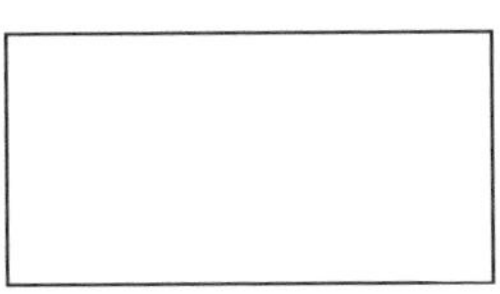

H 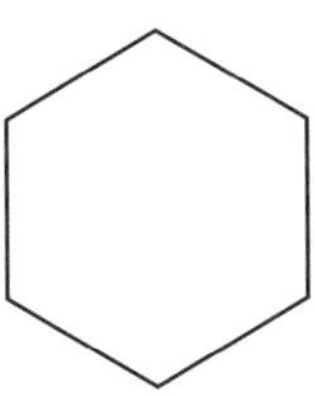

I 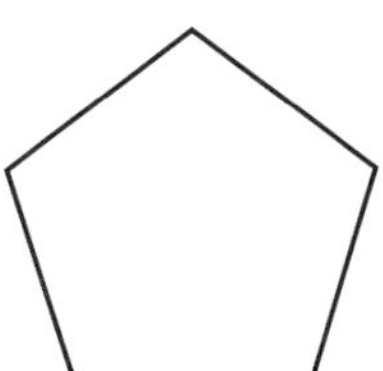

Matching—Shapes

Match the names with the shapes.

1. 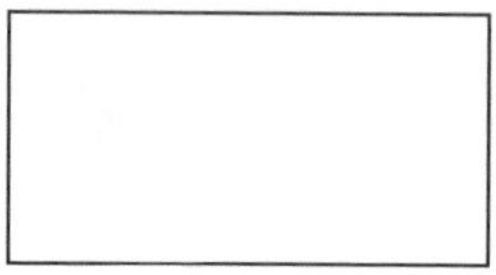

2. 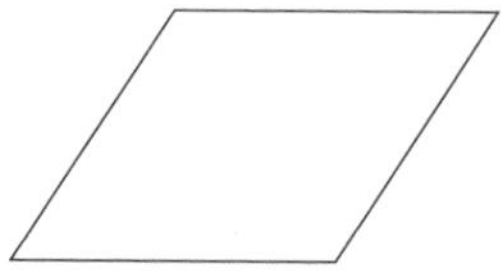

3. 

4. 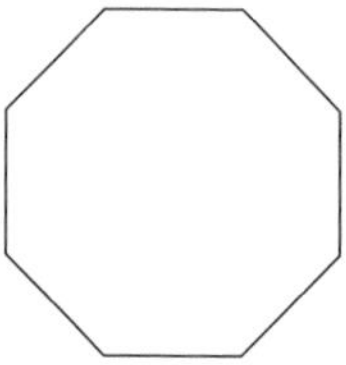

5. 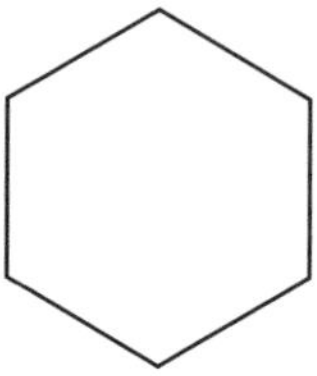

6. 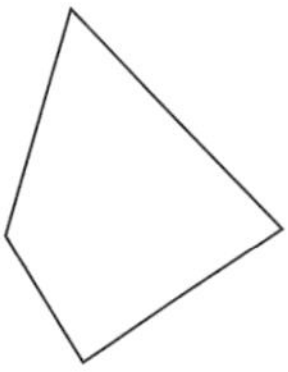

7. 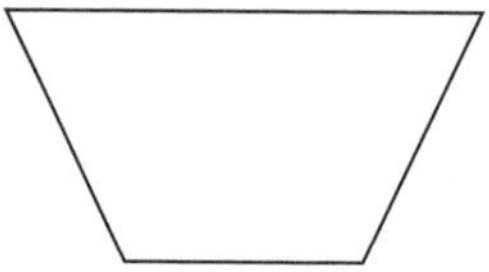

8. 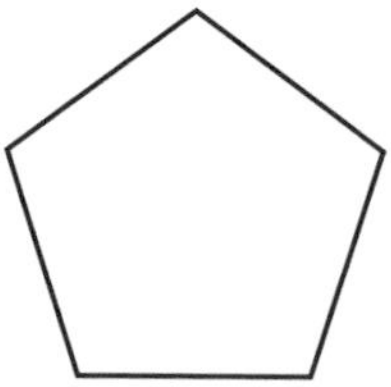

9. 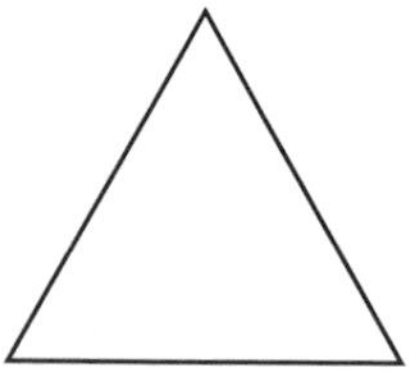

A. ______ pentagon

B. ______ square

C. ______ rectangle

D. ______ triangle

E. ______ quadrilateral

F. ______ parallelogram

G. ______ hexagon

H. ______ octagon

I. ______ trapezoid

Matching—Definitions

Match the name to the definition.

1. pentagon
2. parallelogram
3. square
4. hexagon
5. rectangle
6. octagon
7. triangle
8. trapezoid
9. quadrilateral
10. polygon

A. ______ a polygon with six sides

B. ______ a quadrilateral with opposite sides parallel and congruent

C. ______ a polygon with three angles

D. ______ a plane figure in which all angles are right angles; opposite sides are parallel, and opposite angles are equal

E. ______ a rectangle with all four sides equal; opposite sides are parallel, and opposite angles are equal

F. ______ a five-sided polygon

G. ______ a figure made up of three or more line segments connected so that the area is closed in

H. ______ an eight-sided polygon

I. ______ any four-sided figure

J. ______ a quadrilateral with two sides not parallel and two sides parallel

Matching—Space Figures

Match the names with the shapes.

1.

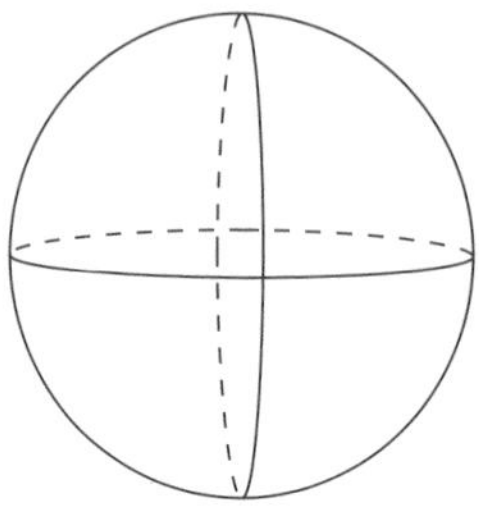

2.

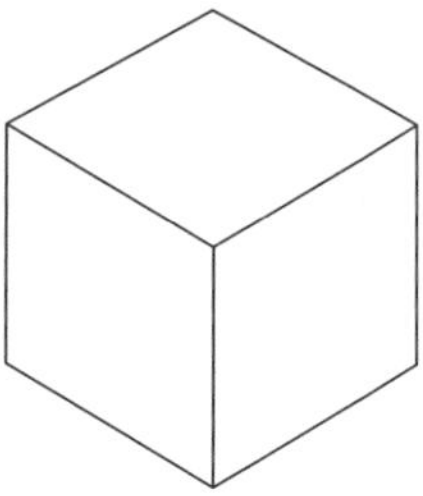

3.

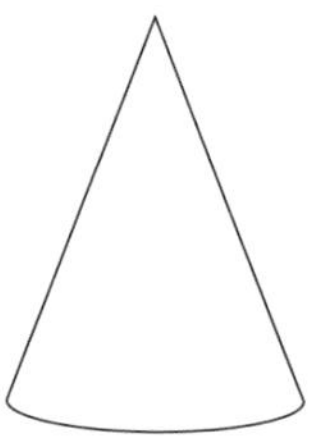

4.

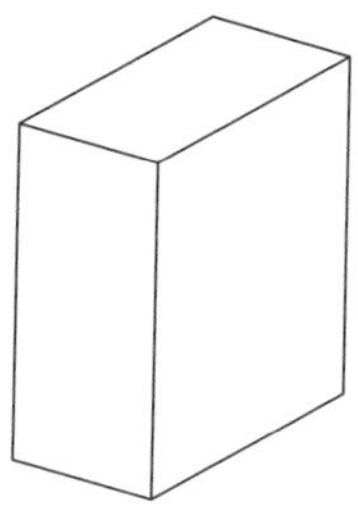

5.

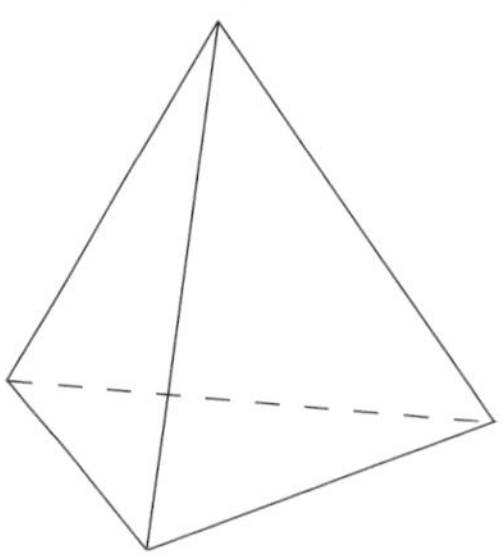

6.

A. _____ rectangular prism

B. _____ cube

C. _____ triangular pyramid

D. _____ sphere

E. _____ cone

F. _____ cylinder

Drawing Shapes

Draw the following three-dimensional shapes.

1. cube

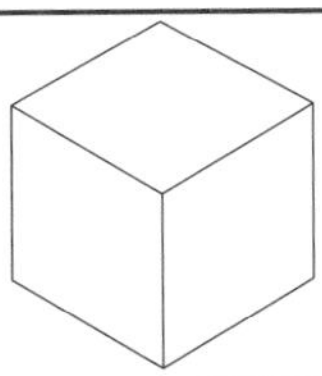

2. cylinder

3. sphere

4. cone

5. rectangular prism

6. triangular pyramid

Matching—Terms to Shapes

Match the name to the example.

A. parallel lines ____

B. perpendicular lines ____

C. vertex ____

D. face ____

E. edge ____

F. ray ____

G. line segment ____

H. angle ____

1.

2.

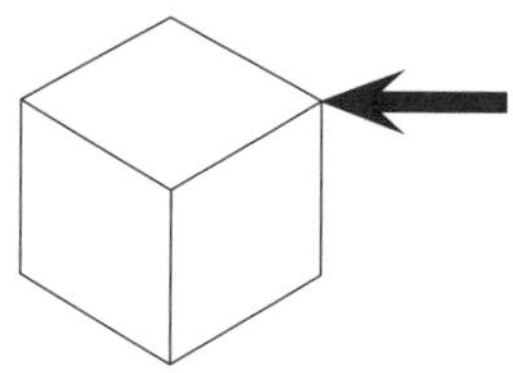

3.

4.

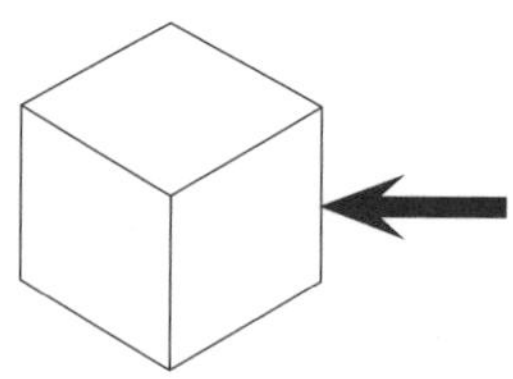

5.

6.

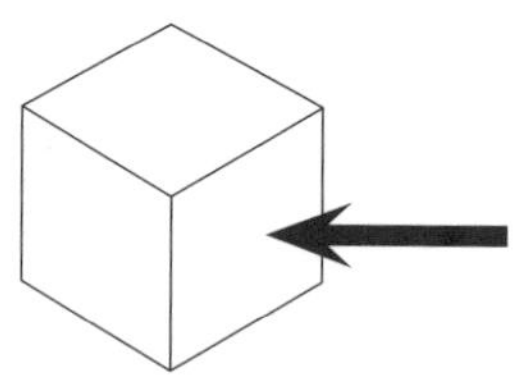

7.

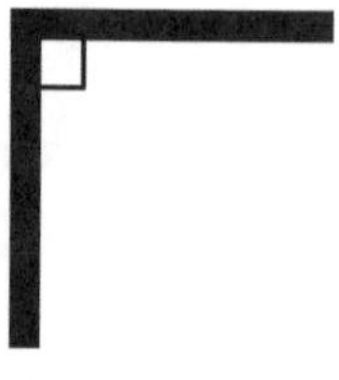

8.

Matching—Lines, Angles, and Faces

Draw a line connecting the name to the definition.

1. parallel lines	lines that never intersect
2. perpendicular lines	lines that intersect to form four right angles
3. vertex	a flat surface of a solid figure
4. face	a line segment where two or more faces of a solid figure meet
5. edge	the endpoint of three line segments on a solid figure
6. ray	the space between two nonparallel rays that share an endpoint
7. line segment	lines that cross each other at only one point
8. angle	a line with two endpoints
9. intersecting lines	a line that has one endpoint and continues on in one direction

What's Your Name?

Tell whether the polygon is regular or not. Write **regular** or **not regular**.

Example:

A **polygon** is a closed plane figure with straight sides that is named by the number of its sides and angles.
A **regular** polygon has all **sides** the same length!

1.

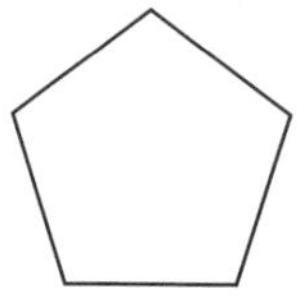

regular ____________________

2.

____

3.

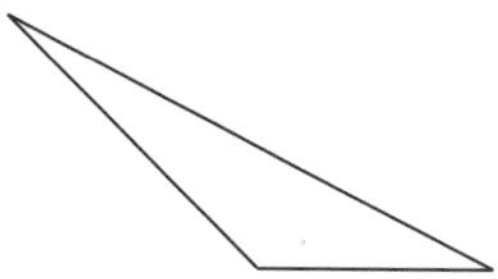

____

4.

____

5.

____

6.

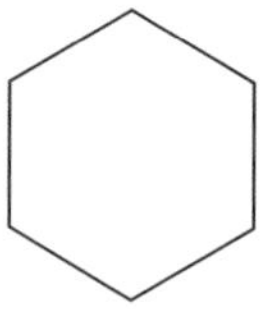

____

7.

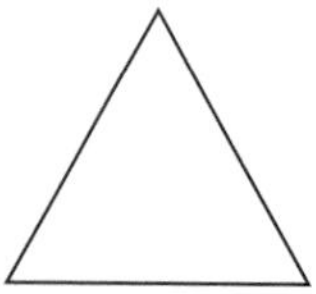

____

8.

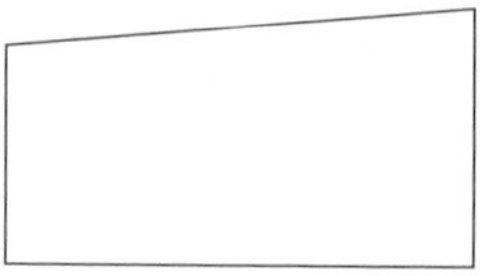

____

Picture the Polygons

Draw the shape described in the box.

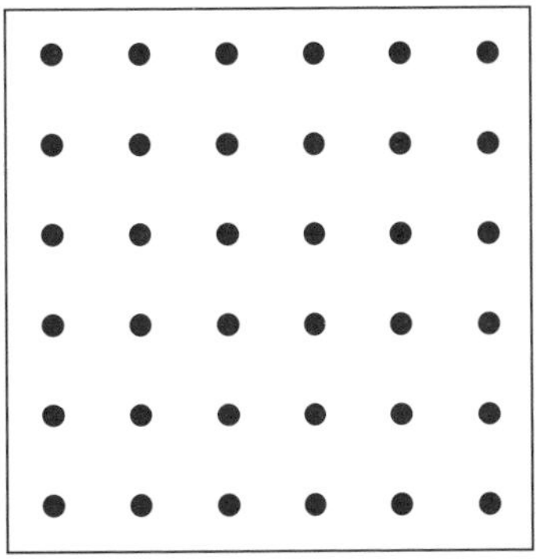

This triangle has three sides.

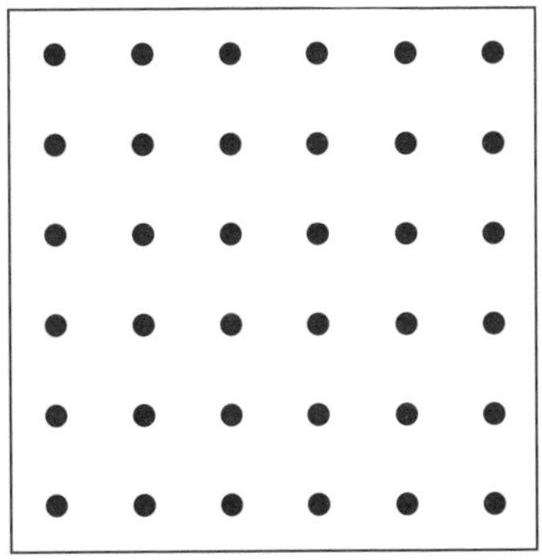

This quadrilateral has four sides.

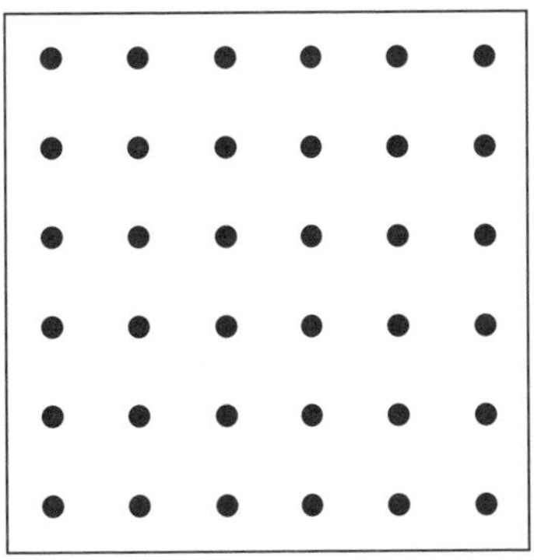

This pentagon has five sides.

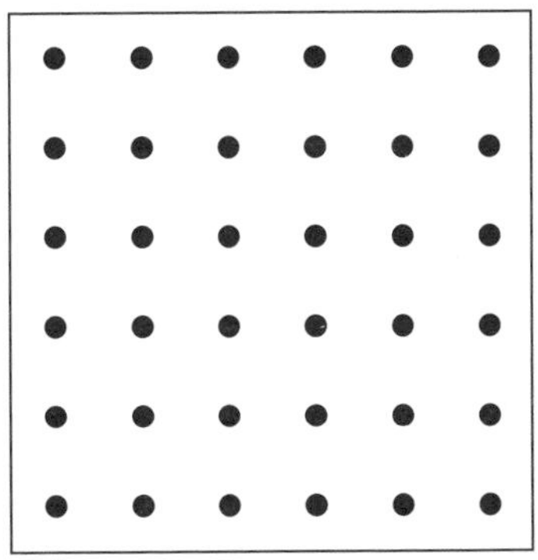

This hexagon has six sides.

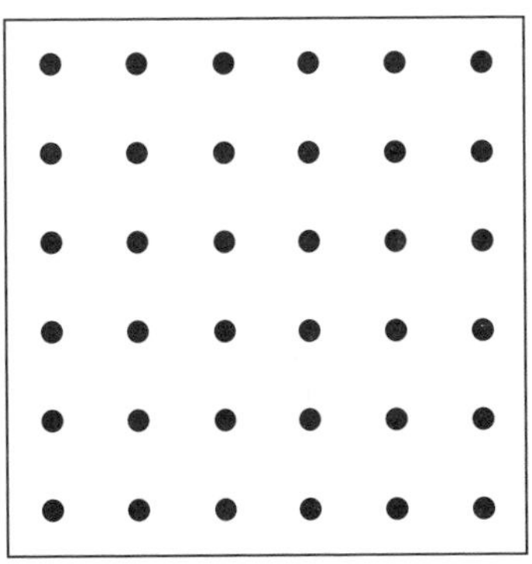

This octagon has eight sides.

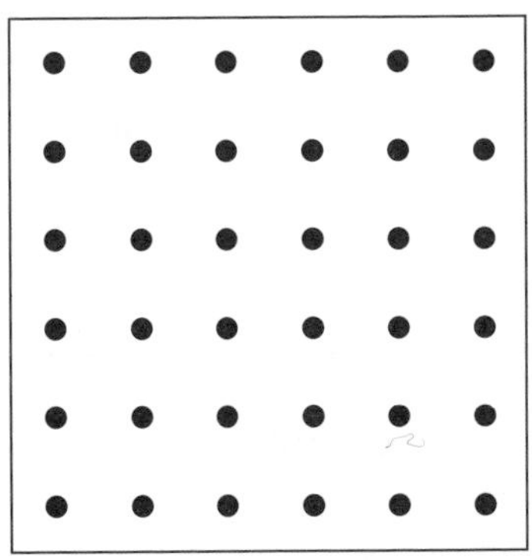

This decagon has ten sides.

Who Am I?

Use the hints to guess the shape, and draw it in the space provided.

Hint	Shape Name	Draw the Shape
Example: I have four sides. Two are parallel, and two are not parallel.	**trapezoid**	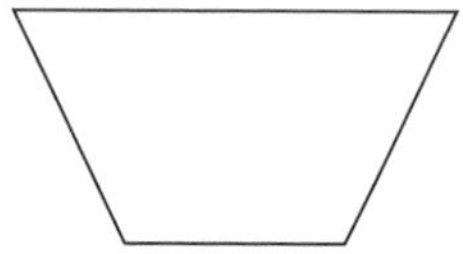
1. All four of my sides are equal.		
2. My opposite sides are equal and parallel. I have four right angles. I am not a square.		
3. I am a polygon with six sides and six angles.		
4. I have two perpendicular lines, with three angles.		
5. I have two pairs of perpendicular lines, two right angles, and five sides.		

Word Problems—Plane Shapes

Solve each problem. Some shapes will be used in more than one answer.

1. I am a quadrilateral with four congruent sides and no right angles. What am I?

____

2. I am a quadrilateral with opposite sides parallel, and I have four right angles. What am I?

____

3. I have two pairs of congruent sides and two pairs of parallel sides. Two angles are acute, and two are obtuse.What type of quadrilateral am I?

____

4. I have four sides and four angles. Two angles are acute, and two are obtuse. What figure could I be?

____

5. Four of my sides are congruent, and I have four right angles. What type of quadrilateral am I?

____

6. I am a quadrilateral with opposite sides congruent and two pairs of right angles. What am I?

____

Mix and Match

Solve each problem.

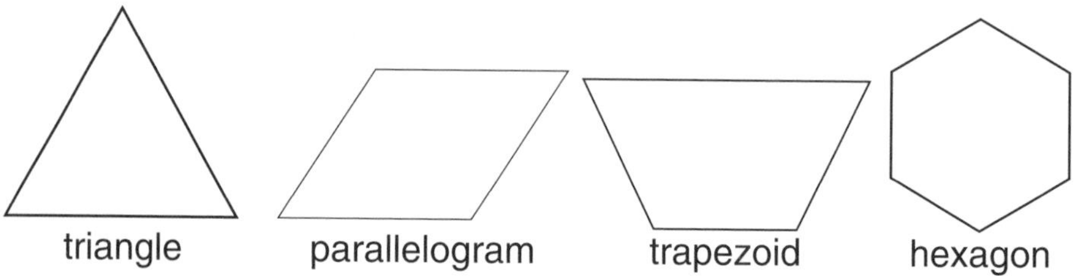

1. How many triangles make up a parallelogram?
   2

2. How many triangles make up a trapezoid?

3. How many triangles make up a hexagon?

4. What combination of shapes could you use to make a trapezoid?

5. What combination of shapes could you use to make a hexagon?

6. List another combination of shapes that you could use to make a hexagon?

Shapes in Your City

Below are signs that you might see in your city. Next to each sign write the name of the shape.

1.

____

2.

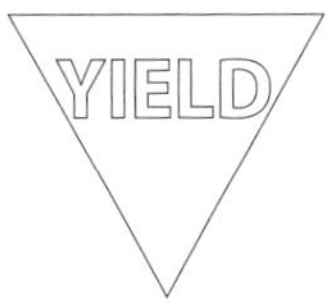

____

3.

____

4.

____

5.

____

6.

____

7.

____

It All Adds Up

Find the perimeter for each shape.

Remember: To find the perimeter, add all of the sides of the shape together.

1.

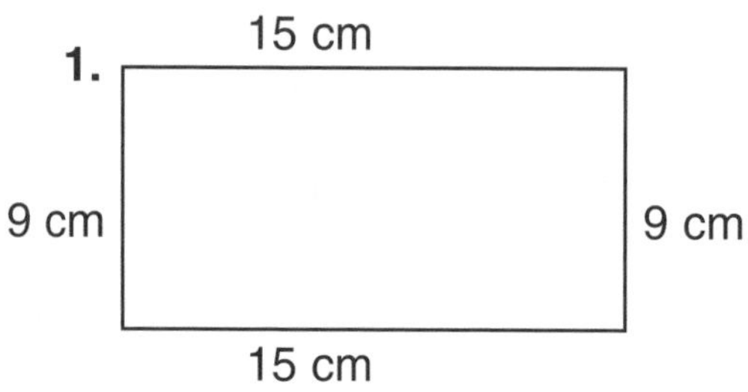

2.

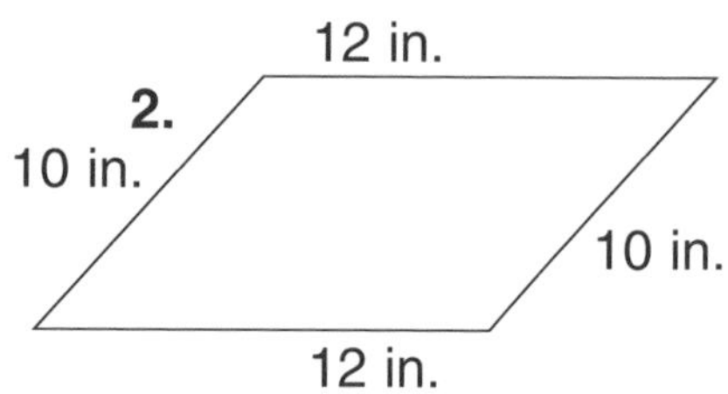

3.

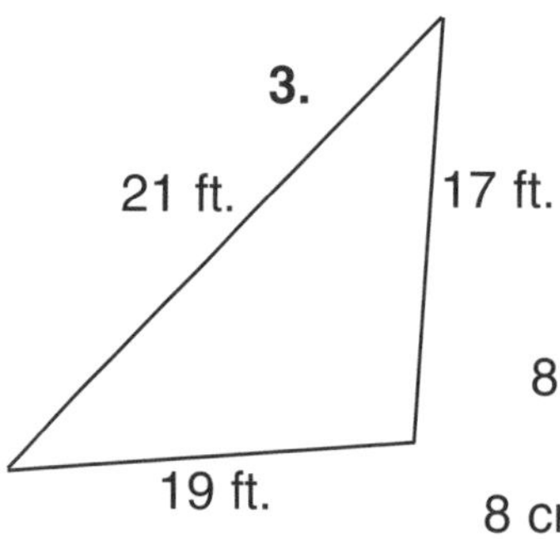

4.

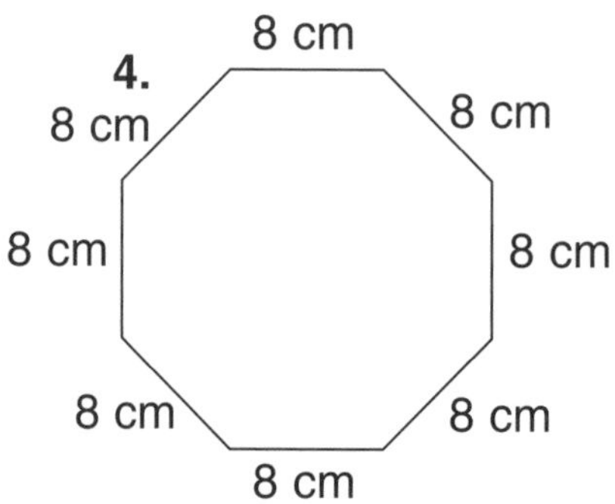

5.

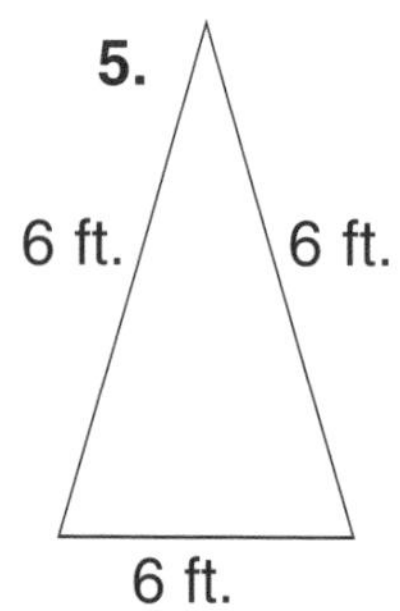

6.

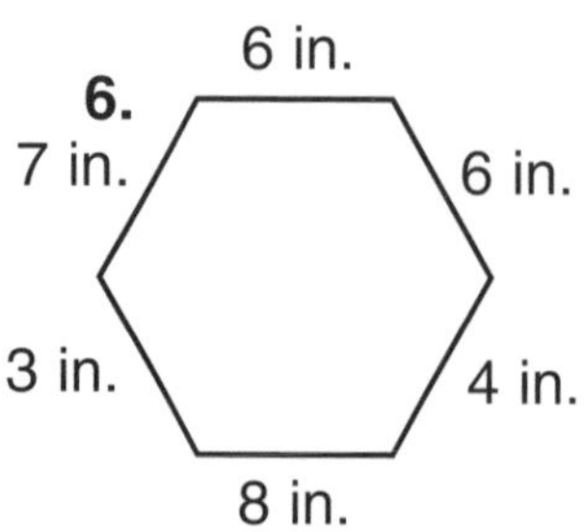

7.

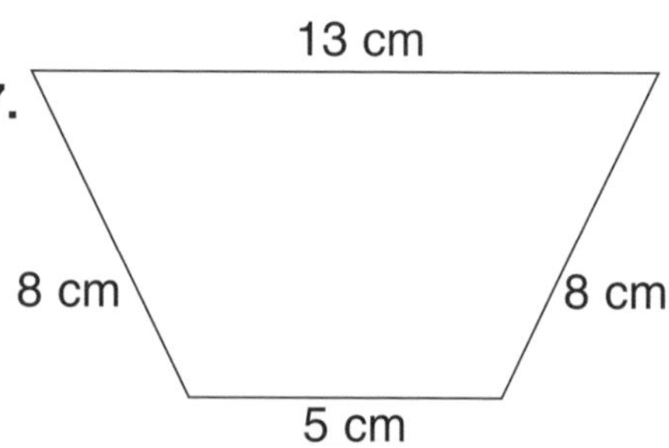

Multiplying to Find the Perimeter

Use the formula **P = (2 x L) + (2 x H)** to find the perimeter of a quadrilateral with opposite sides equal. Use the steps shown in the example.

Remember: You find the perimeter by adding all of the sides together, OR you can use this formula for quadrilaterals with opposite sides equal:
P = (2 x L) + (2 x H).

Example:

1. P = (2 x **12**) + (2 x **3**)
P = (2 x 12) + (2 x 3)
P = 24 + 6
P = 30 in.

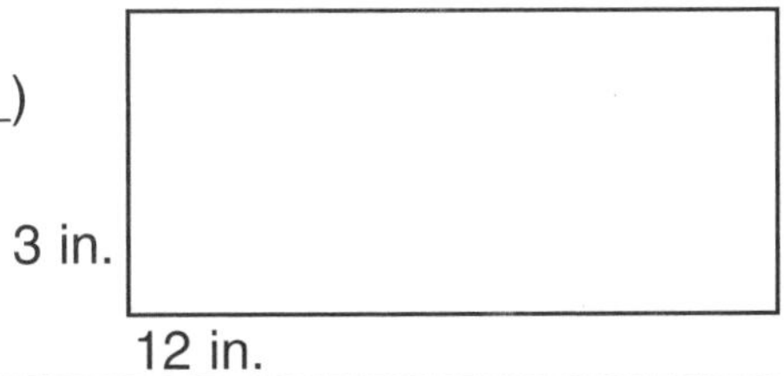

2. P = (2 x ____) + (2 x ____)
P = (2 x ____) + (2 x ____)
P = ____ + ____
P = ______

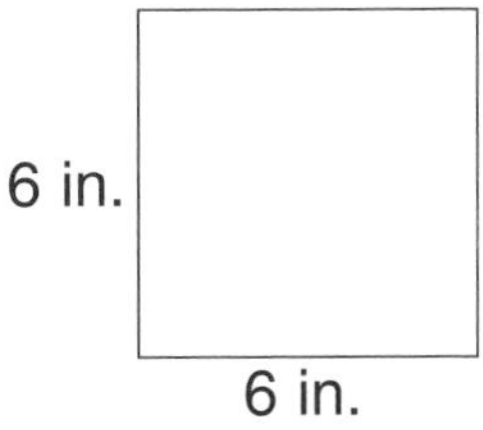

3. P = (2 x ____) + (2 x ____)
P = (2 x ____) + (2 x ____)
P = ____ + ____

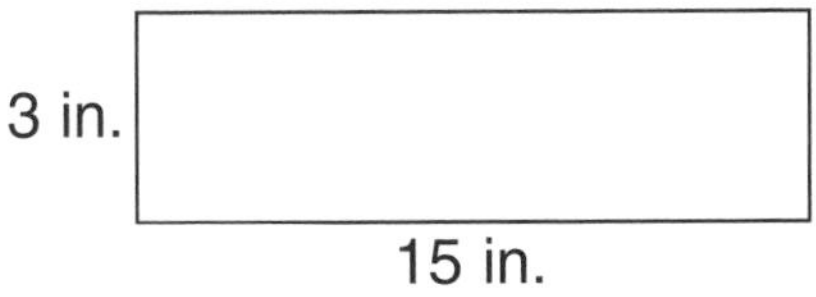

4. P = (2 x ____) + (2 x ____)
P = (2 x ____) + (2 x ____)

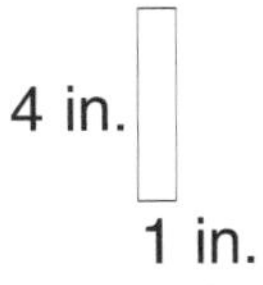

5. P = (2 x ____) + (2 x ____)

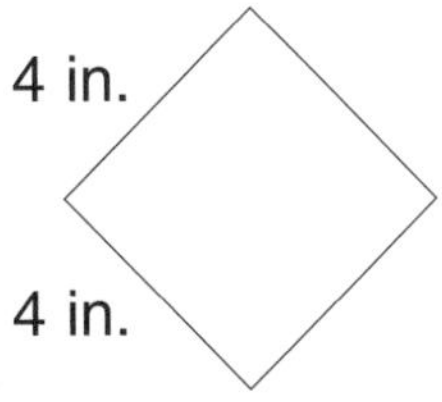

Counting Perimeters

Look at each shape. Count how many units form the perimeter.

Example:

16 units

1	2	3	4	5
16				6
15				7
14				8
13	12	11	10	9

1.

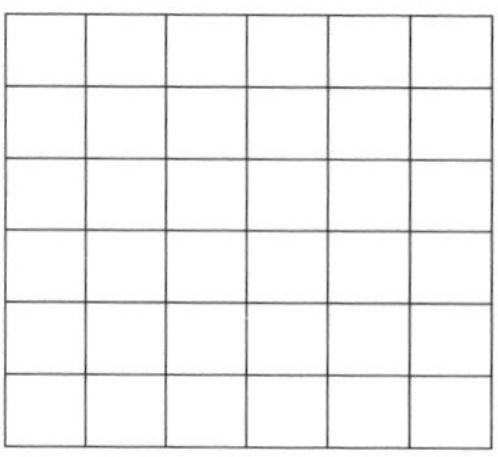

2.

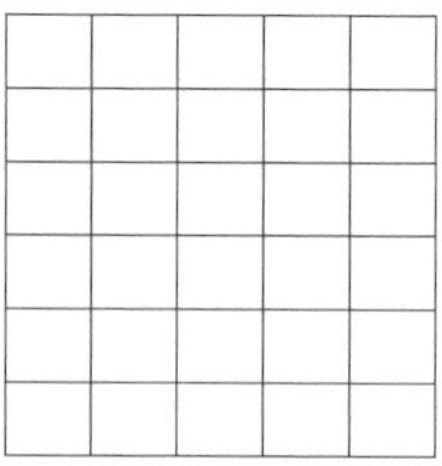

3.

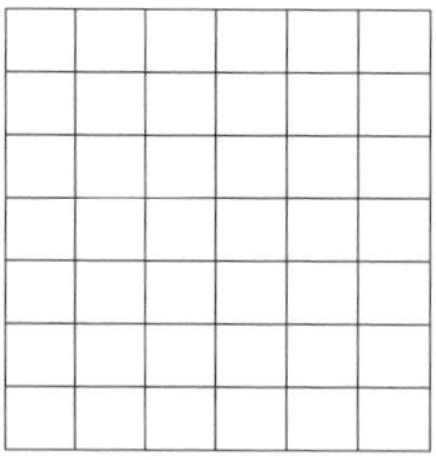

4.

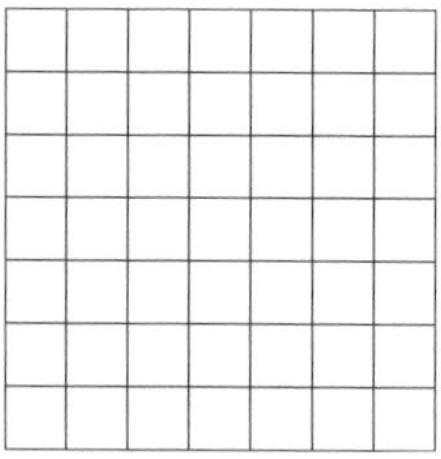

5.

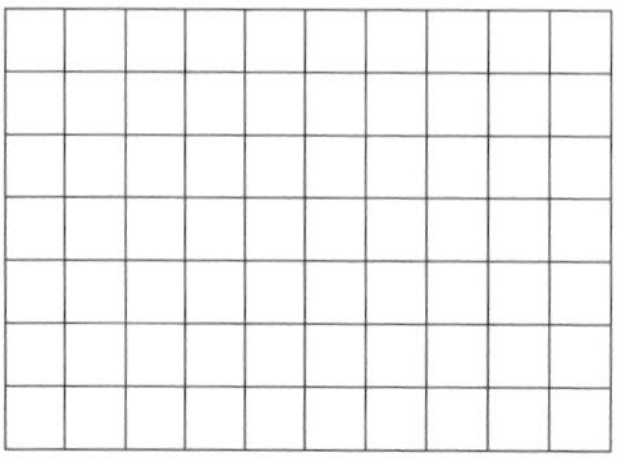

6.

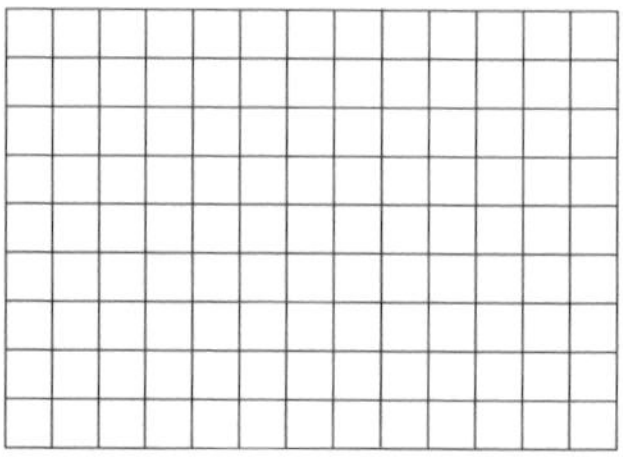

Problem Solving—Perimeter

Solve each problem.

1. Mrs. Johansen's pool is a rectangle 24 feet long and 13 feet wide. What is the perimeter of her pool?

   The perimeter of the pool is ____________________ feet.

2. The rectangular table is 24 inches long and 15 inches wide. What is the perimeter of the tabletop?

   The perimeter of the tabletop is_______________ inches.

3. A playground is rectangular. The sides are 280 feet long and 124 feet wide. What is the perimeter of the playground?

   The perimeter of the playground is ______________ feet.

4. The garden is a rectangle. It is 14 feet long and 13 feet wide. How much fencing will you need to go around the garden?

   The garden needs ______ feet of fencing.

5. The rectangular mirror is 28 inches wide and 36 inches long. What is the perimeter of the mirror?

   The perimeter of the mirror is ________________ inches.

Use the space below to **draw** and **label** the rectangles if needed.

Perimeter Riddle

Solve the riddle by finding the perimeter of each figure below. Write the letter that represents each problem above its answer.

Riddle: Where does the crab spider live?

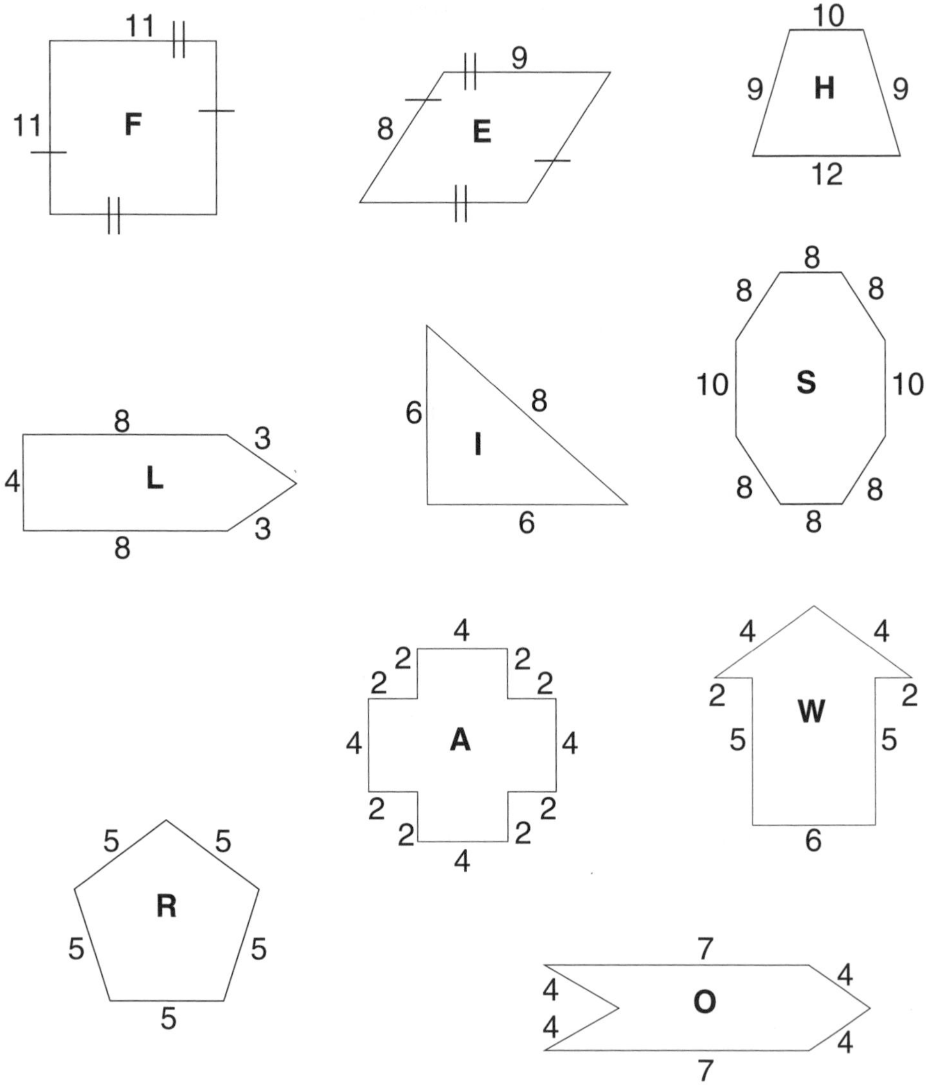

___ ___ ___ ___ ___ ___ ___
44 26 30 28 34 25 68

There's a Lot of Area in That Shape

The **area** is the space inside a shape. To find the area of a regular quadrilateral, you multiply its length by its width: **A = L x W**. Find the area of each of these figures.

Example:

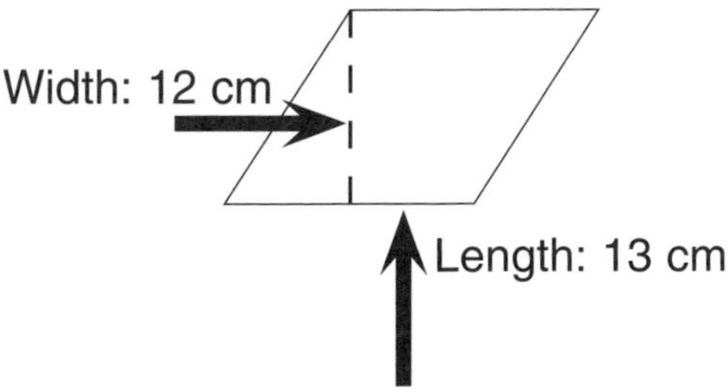

Solve: A = L x W

13 x 12 = ______

$$\begin{array}{r} 13 \\ \underline{x12} \\ \textbf{156 cm} \end{array}$$

1.

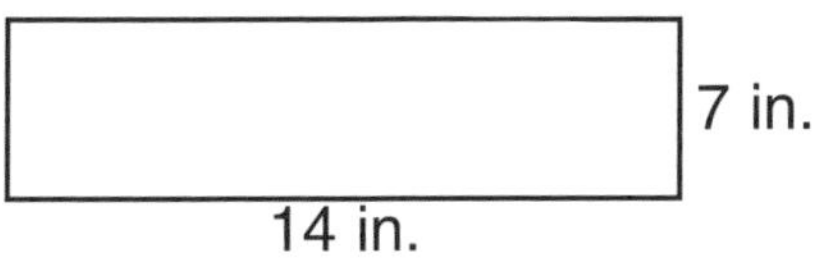

______

2.

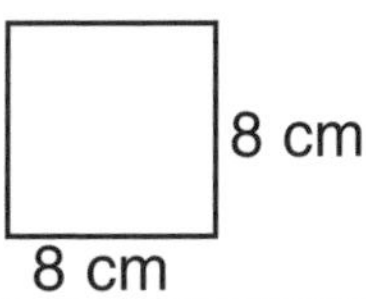

______

3.

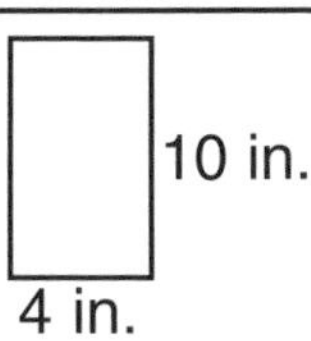

______

4.

______

5.

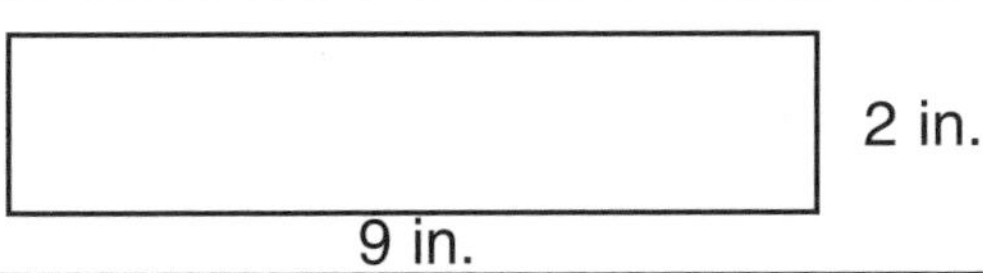

______

6.

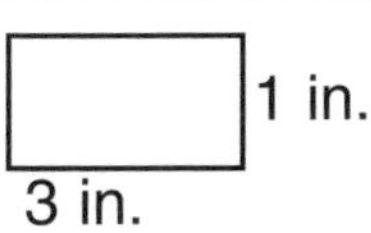

______

Square and Triangle Area

Remember: Area tells the number of square units in a figure.

Find the area of the figures below.

1. 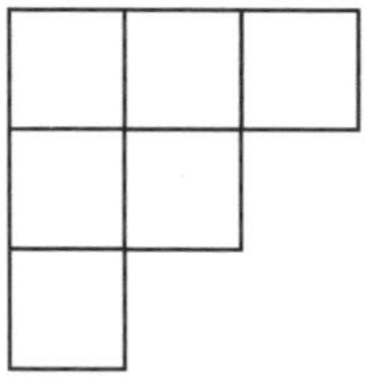

_______ square units

2. 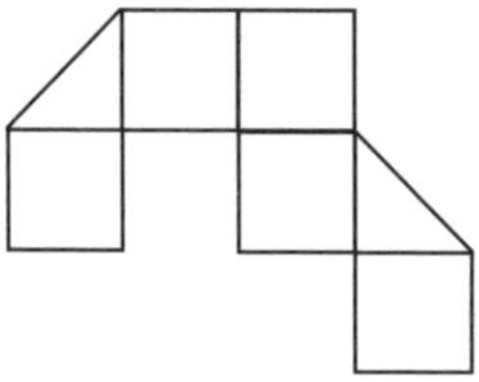

_______ square units

3. 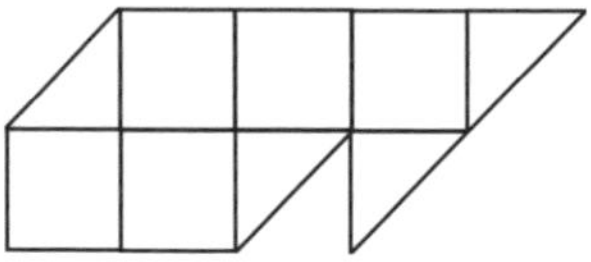

_______ square units

4. 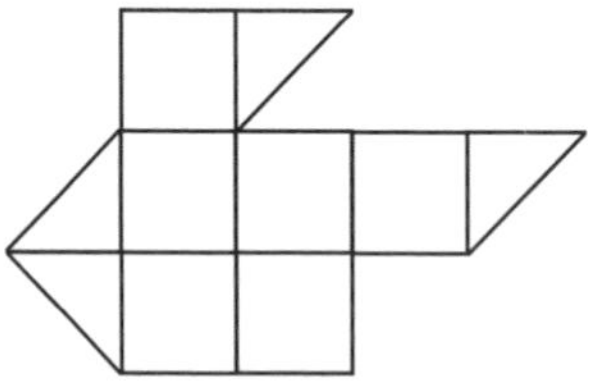

_______ square units

5. 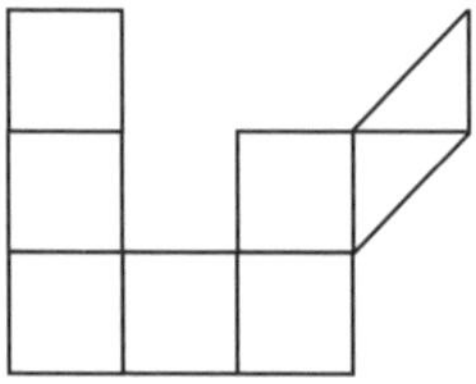

_______ square units

6. 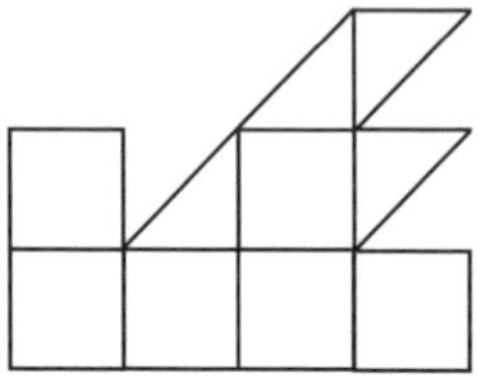

_______ square units

What Area of the House Do You Like Most?

Record the area for each room listed below.

1. bedroom 2 ______

2. master bedroom ______

3. living room ______

4. dining room ______

5. kitchen ______

6. toy room ______

7. What is the largest room? ____________________

8. What is the smallest room? ____________________

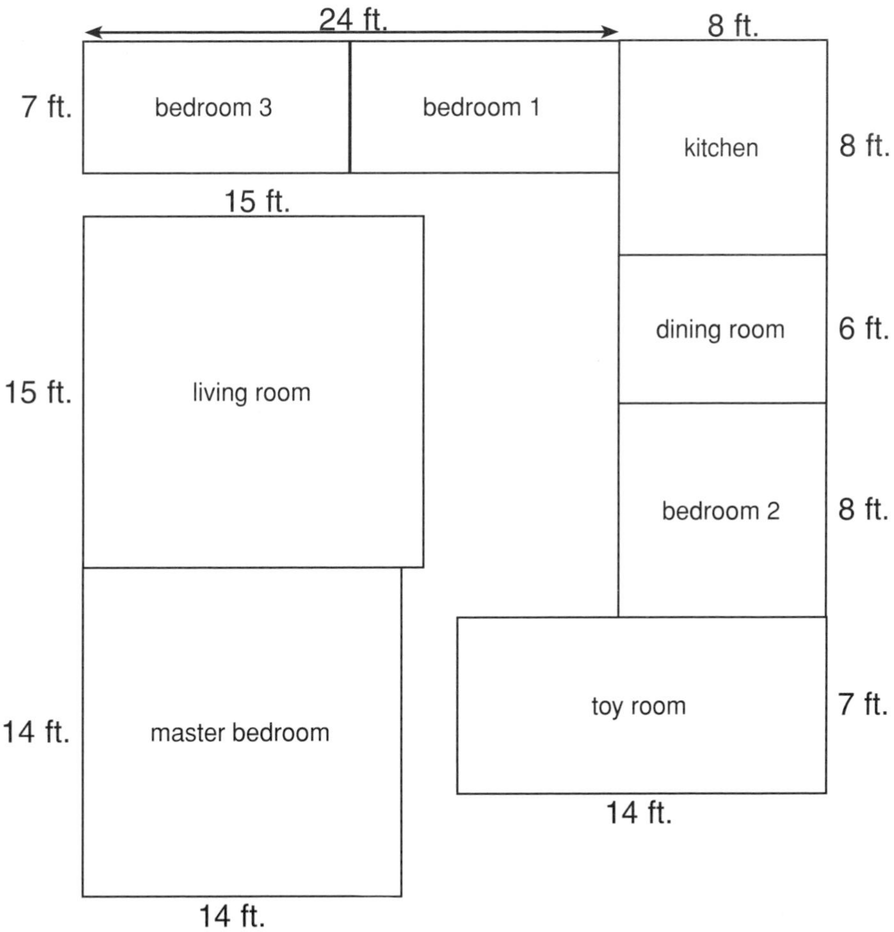

Area Riddle

Solve the riddle by finding the area of each figure below. Write the letter that represents each problem above the answer.

Riddle: What state is closest to the equator?

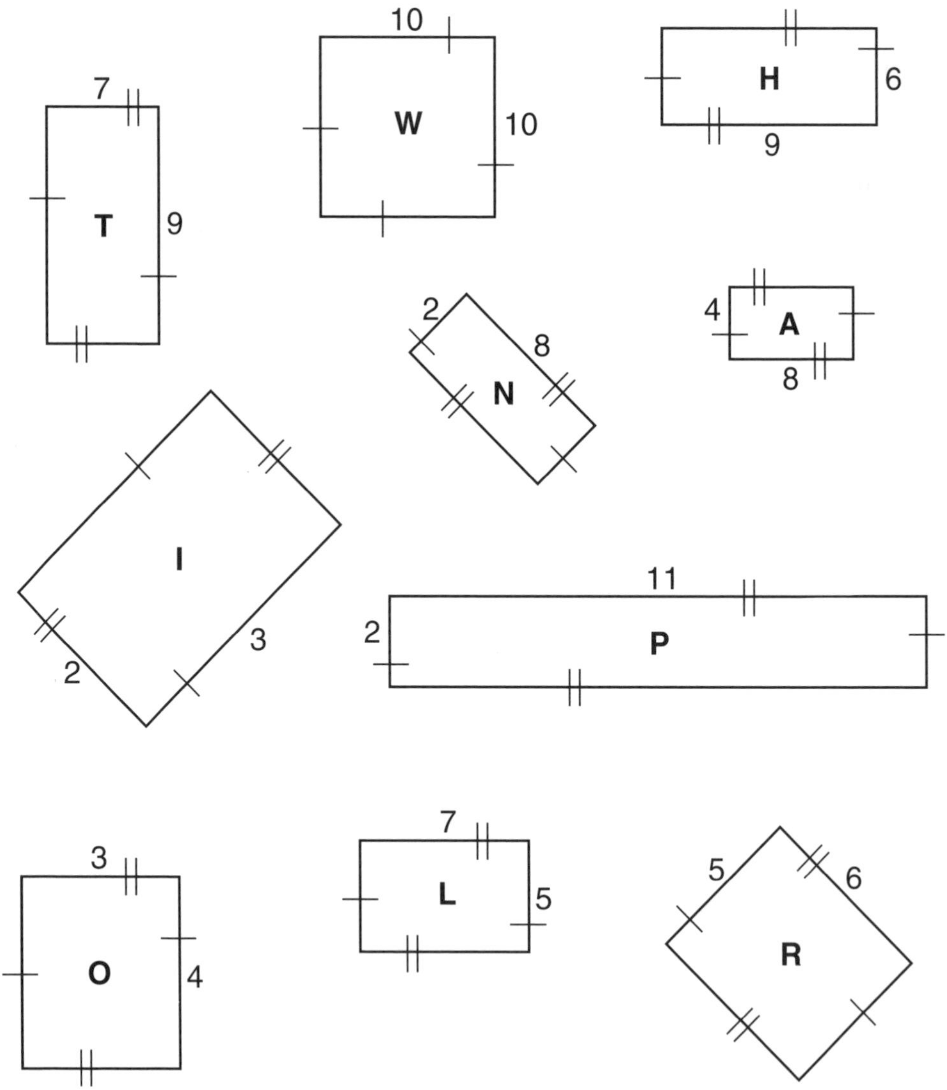

___	___	___	___	___	___
54	32	100	32	6	6

Circles—Terms

Chord—a line segment passing through a circle that has its endpoints on that circle

Circumference—the distance around a circle

Diameter—a chord passing through the center of a circle

Radius—a line segment with one endpoint at the center of a circle and the other endpoint on the circle

Draw an example for each term.

Draw a radius AB.

Trace the circumference.

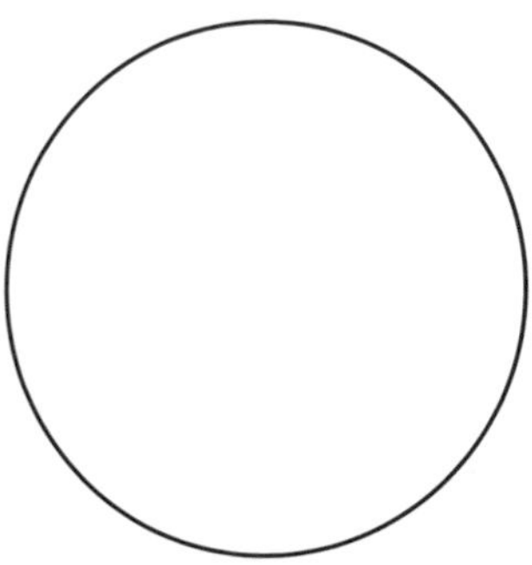

Draw a diameter XY.

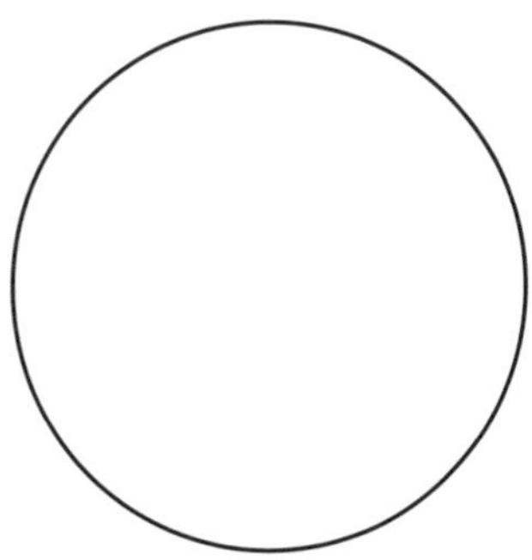

Draw a chord DE.

Circle Graph

Use the drawing to complete the table.

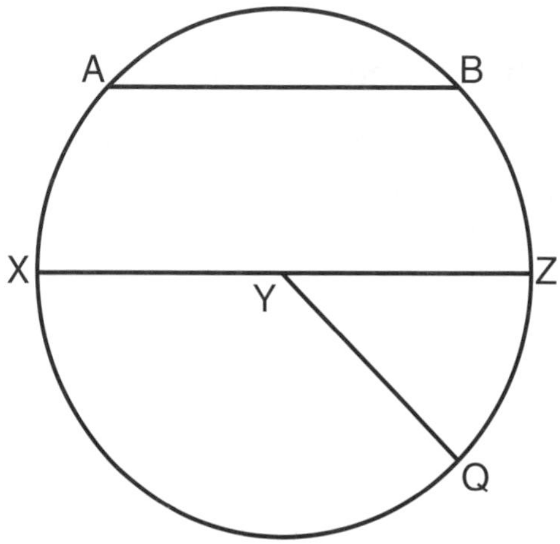

Name	Part of Circle
YQ	**1.**
AB	**2.**
YZ	**3.**
XZ	**4.**

5. The center of the circle is ______________________.

6. Two points on the circle are __________ and __________.

Circle: It Starts in the Center

Solve each problem.

Remember: A circle is named by its center point.

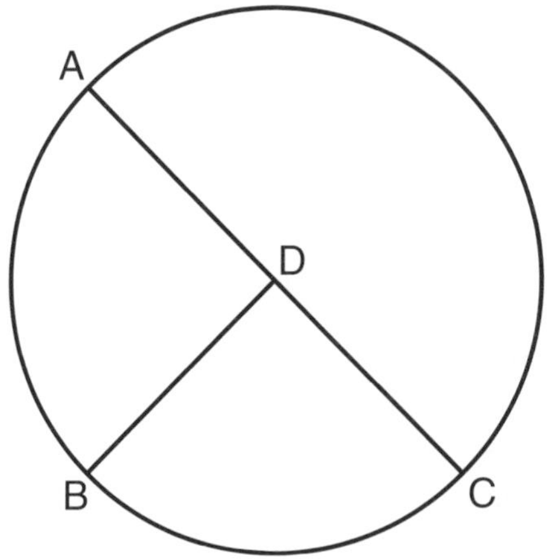

1. A circle is named by its center. What is this circle named?

____

2. Name two radii. ____________________ ____________________

3. Name the diameter. __________________________________

4. Draw another diameter in red and name it EF.

5. Draw two more radii in blue and label them DG and DH.

Three's a Crowd

Estimate the circumference.

Remember: The **circumference** is about 3 times the diameter of the circle. If you know the diameter, you can **estimate** the circumference.

C = (approximately) 3 x diameter

Example:

Diameter is 6 cm.

6 x 3 = 18

The circumference is **about 18 cm**.

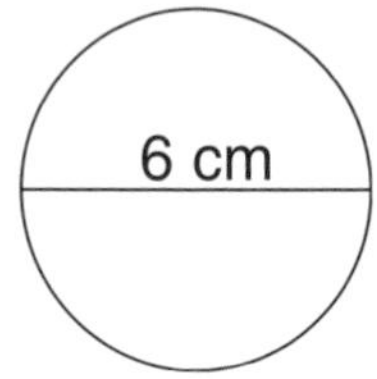

1. Diameter is 4 in.

______ x ______= ________

The circumference is about ________.

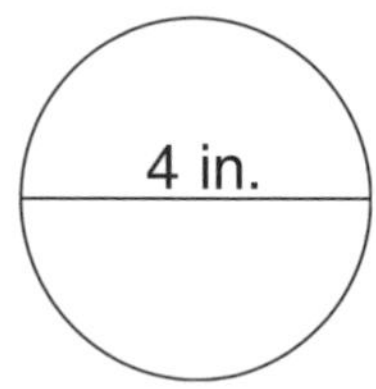

2. Diameter is 9 yd.
Show your work.

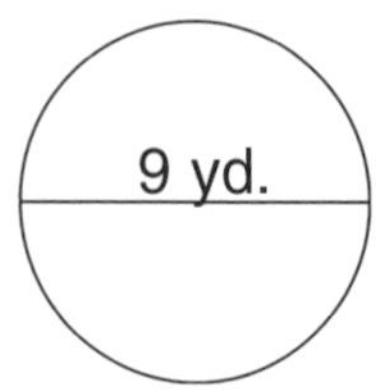

3. Diameter is 12 mm.
Show your work.

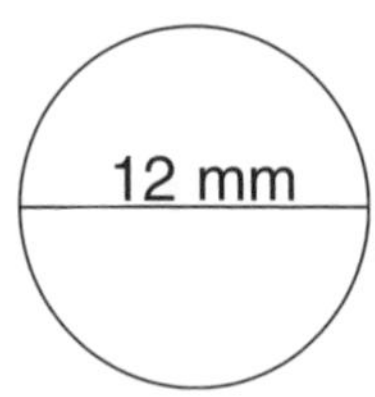

4. Diameter is 8 ft.
Show your work.

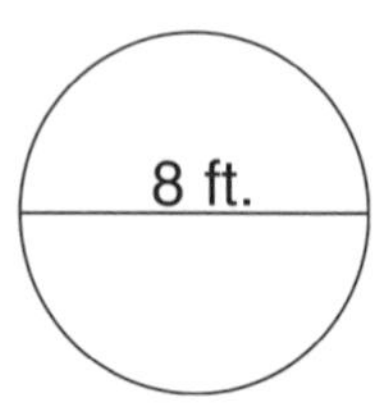

Half or Double the Recipe?

Show your work.

Remember: The **radius** is half the diameter of a circle. To find the diameter, double the radius.

Example:

Find the diameter.
radius x 2 = diameter
4 x 2 = 8
diameter = 8 in.

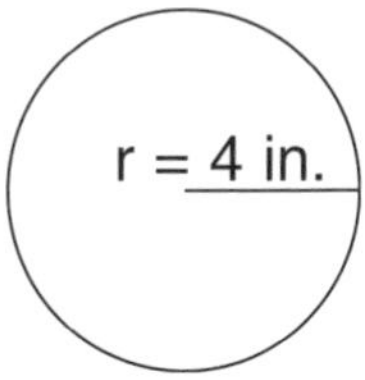

1. Find the diameter.

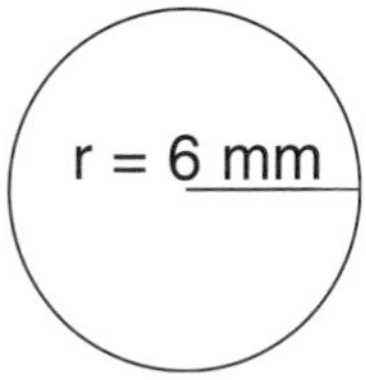

2. Find the diameter.

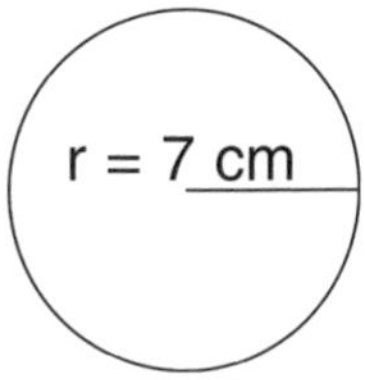

3. Find the radius.
diameter ÷ 2 = radius

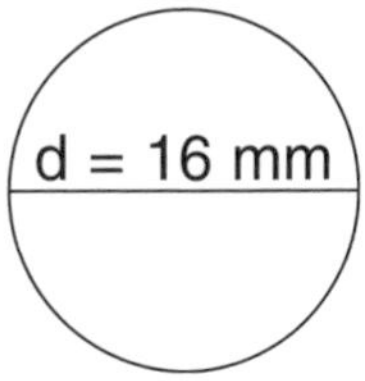

4. Find the radius.

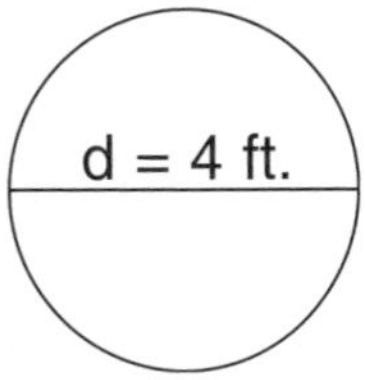

5. Find the radius.

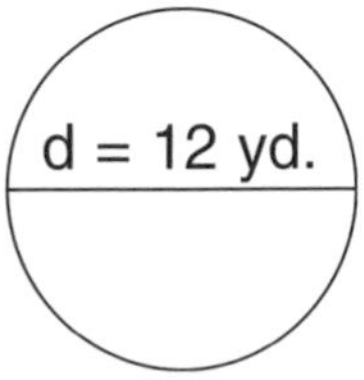

Symmetry

A **line of symmetry** divides a shape into two congruent shapes. **Congruent** shapes are the same shape and size. Identify which shapes have 1 line of symmetry, 2 or more lines of symmetry, or no line of symmetry.

In the space provided write: **1 line of symmetry, 2 or more lines of symmetry**, or **no line of symmetry**.

1. 

2. 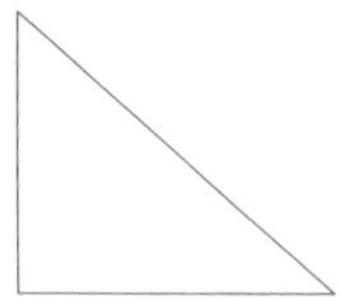

3. 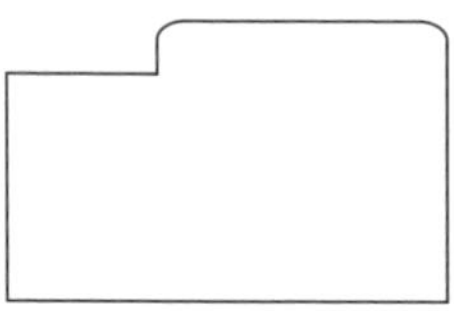

4. 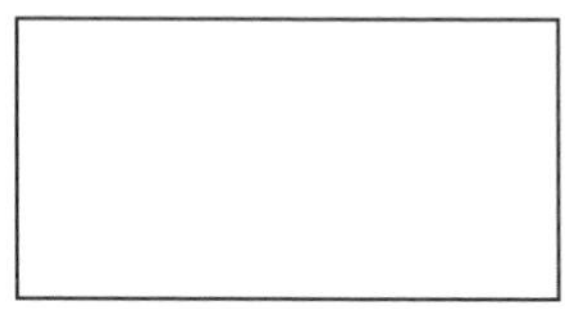

5. 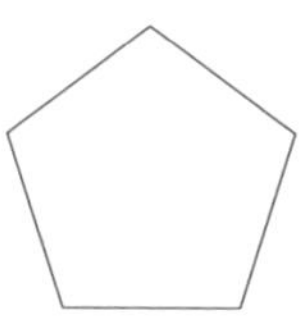

6. 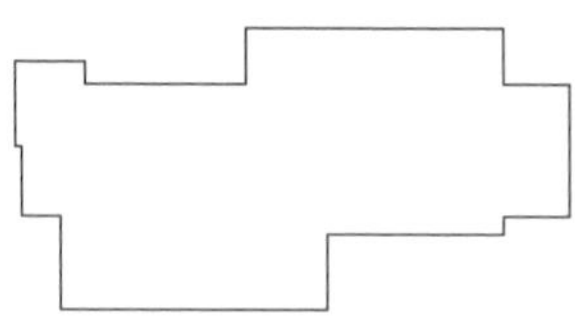

Just Half of the Story

Complete each design to show symmetry. **Remember:** Both sides of the lines of symmetry need to be congruent.

1.

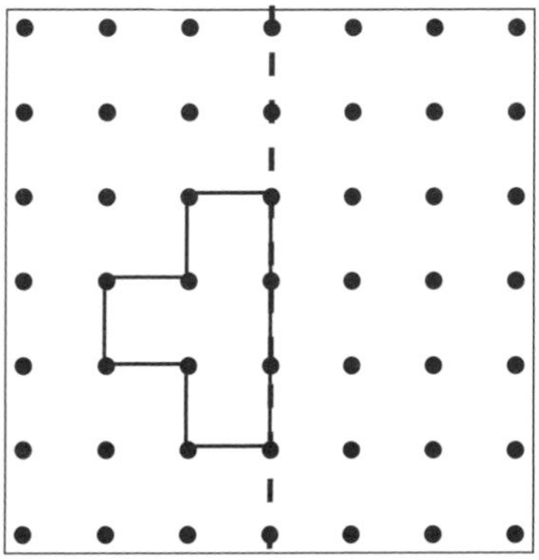

2.

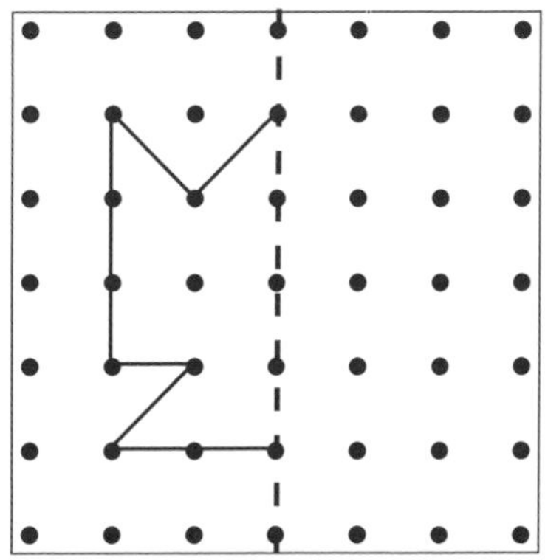

3.

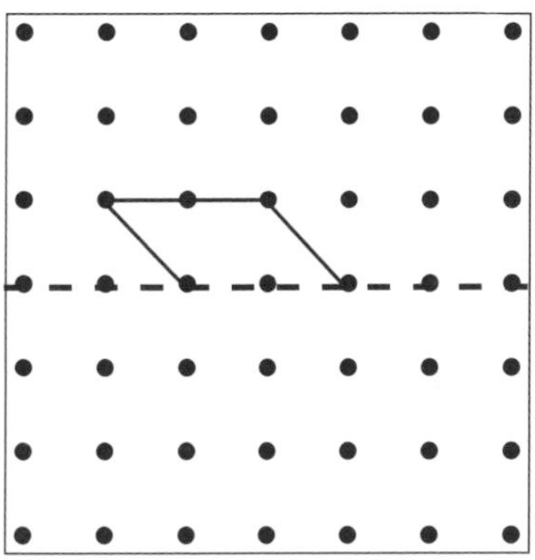

4.

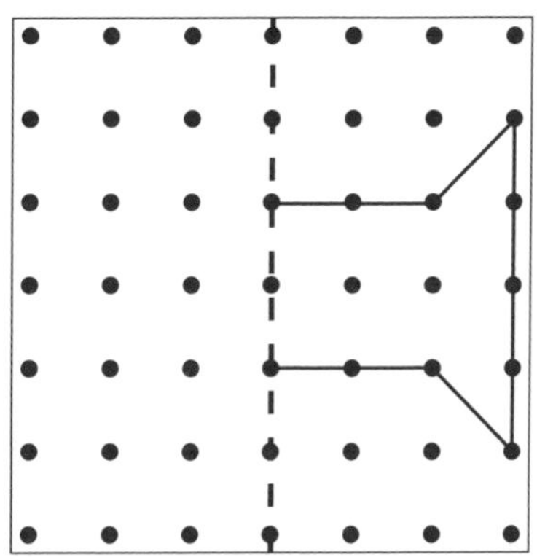

5.

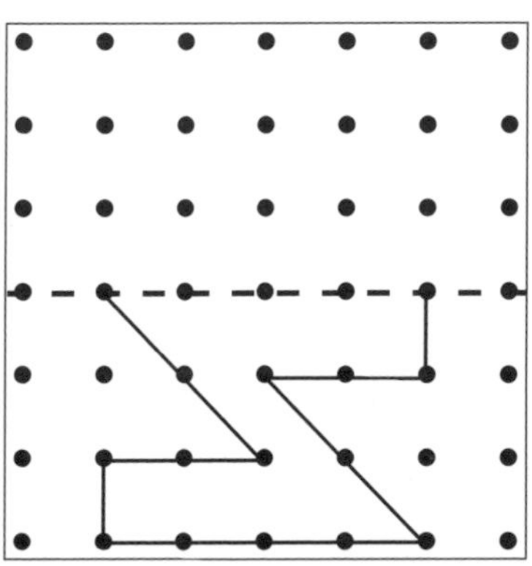

6.

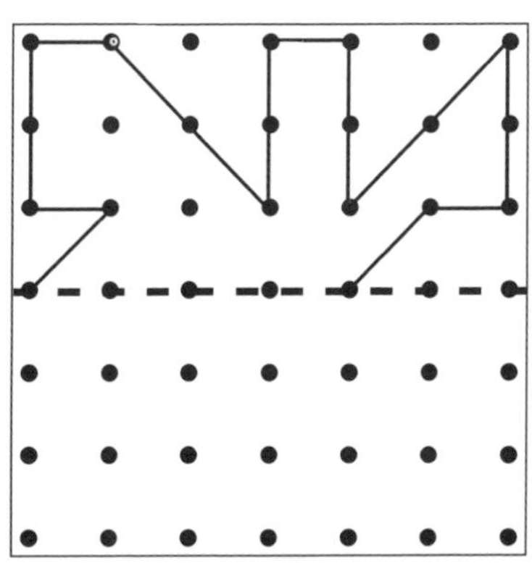

Color the shapes that have the correct line of symmetry.

Remember: A **line of symmetry** divides a shape into two congruent shapes.

1.

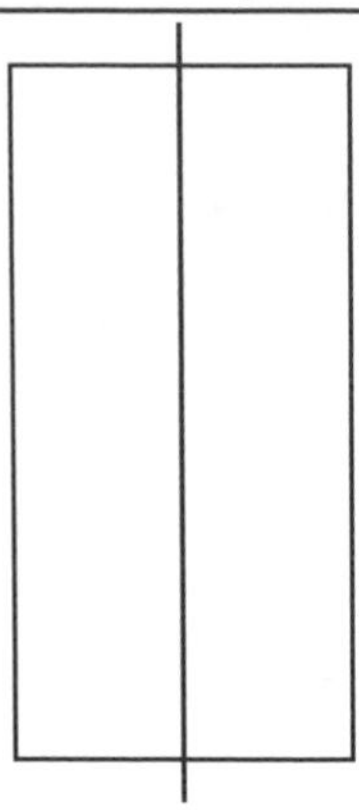

2.

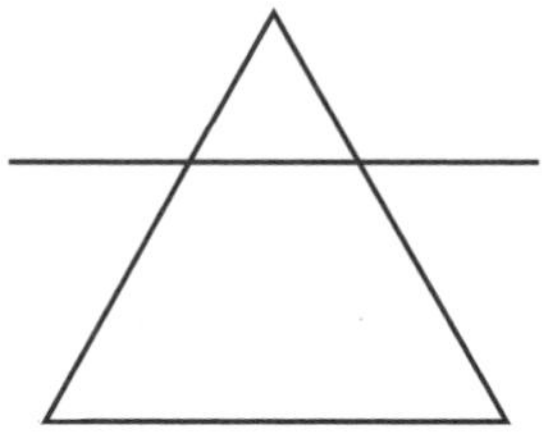

3.

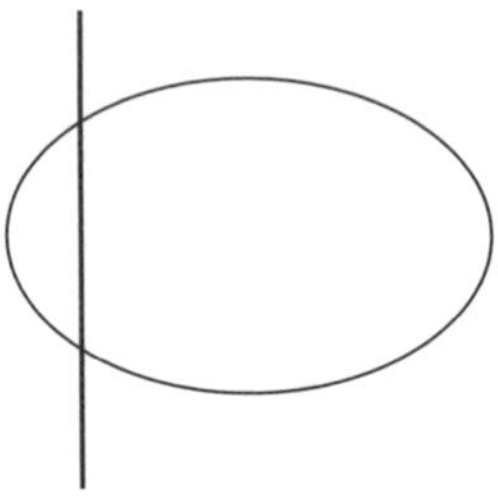

4.

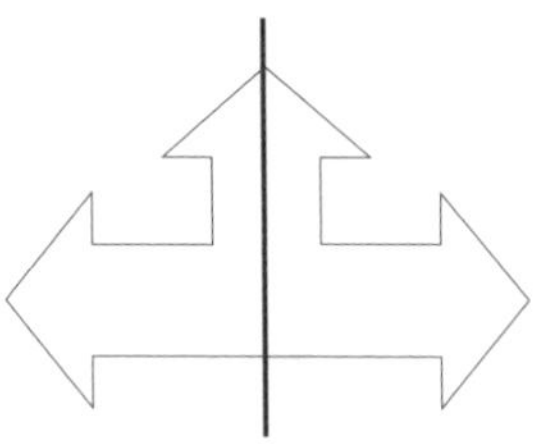

5.

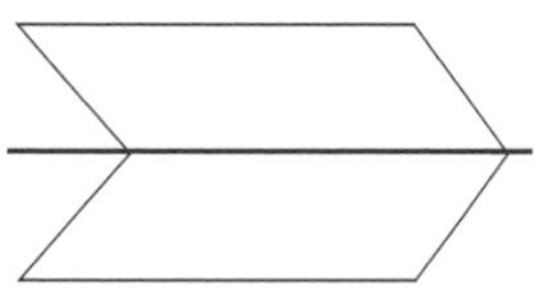

6.

Draw your own shapes with a correct line of symmetry.

7.

8.

9.

Slide—moves a figure to a new position
Turn—rotates a figure around a point
Flip—flips a figure over a line, making a mirror image

List how each figure was moved. Write **flip, turn**, or **slide**.

1.

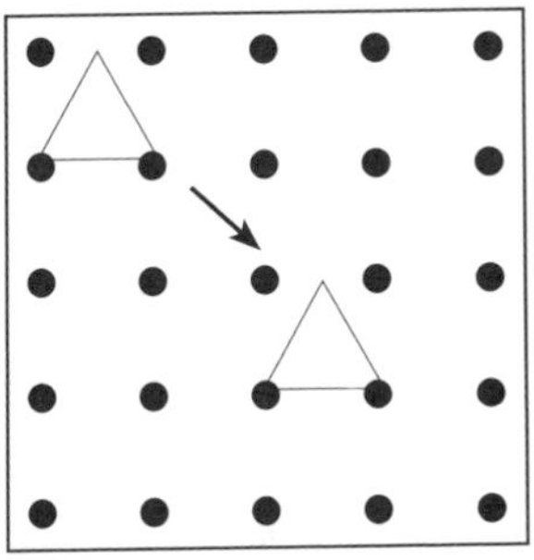

____

2.

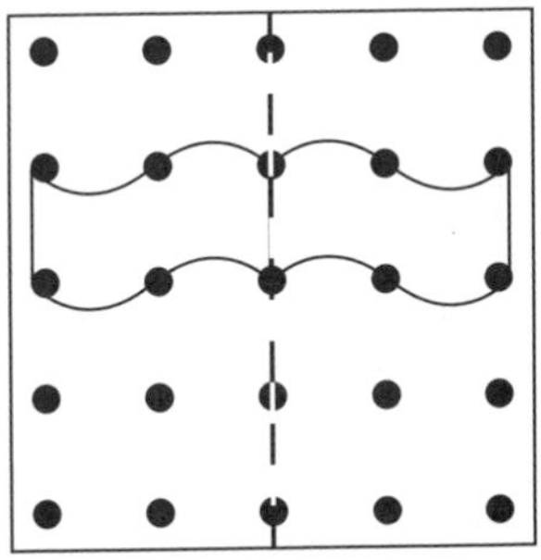

____

3.

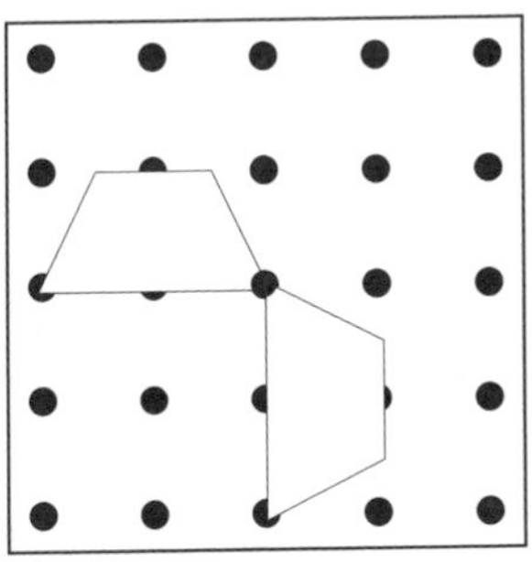

____

4.

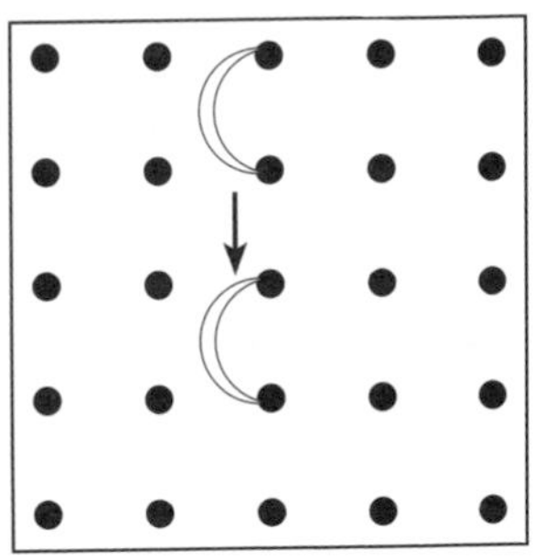

____

5.

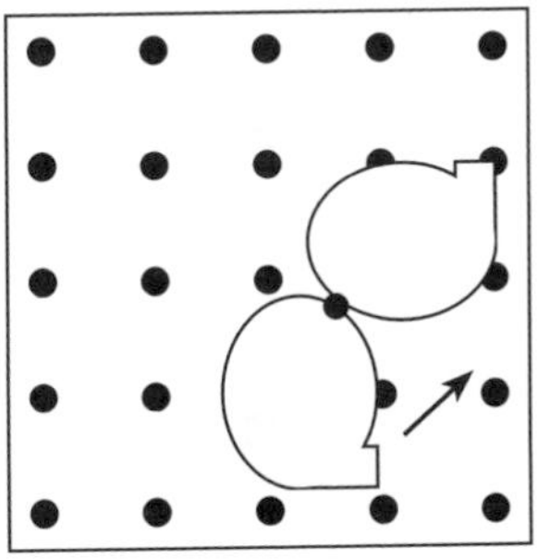

____

6.

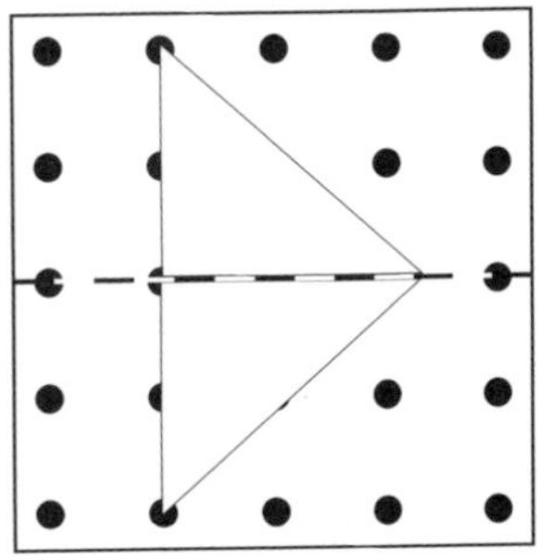

____

One of These Shapes Is Not Like the Others

Circle the two shapes that are congruent.

Example:

A. 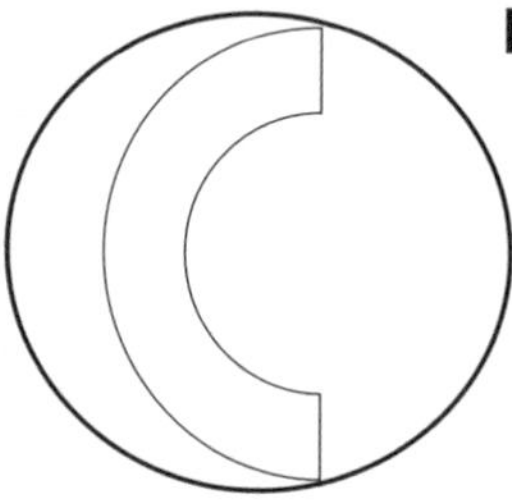

B. 

C. 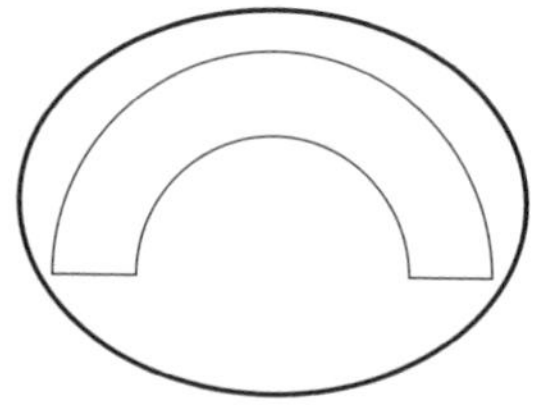

1. A. 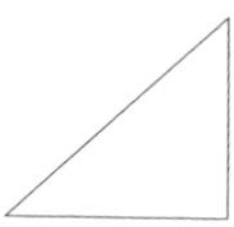 B. 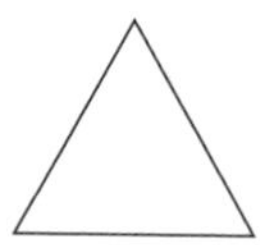 C. 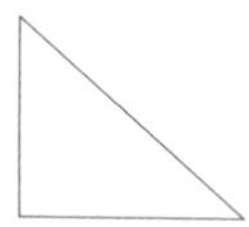

2. A. 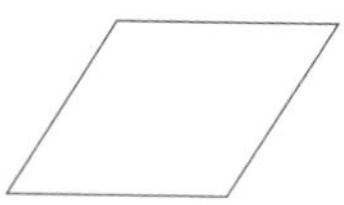 B. 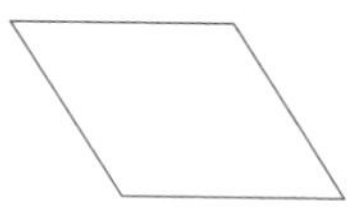 C. 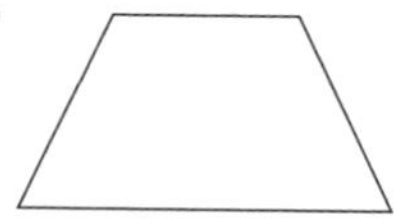

3. A. 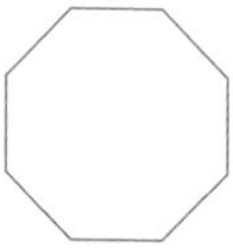 B. 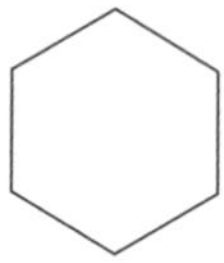 C. 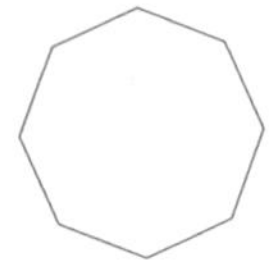

4. A.  B.  C. 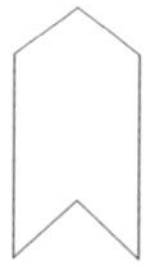

5. A.  B.  C. 

6. A. 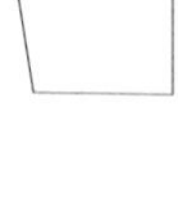 B.  C. 

It's as Easy as Slide, Turn, or Flip

Draw each figure using either a slide, turn, or flip.

Draw a flip.

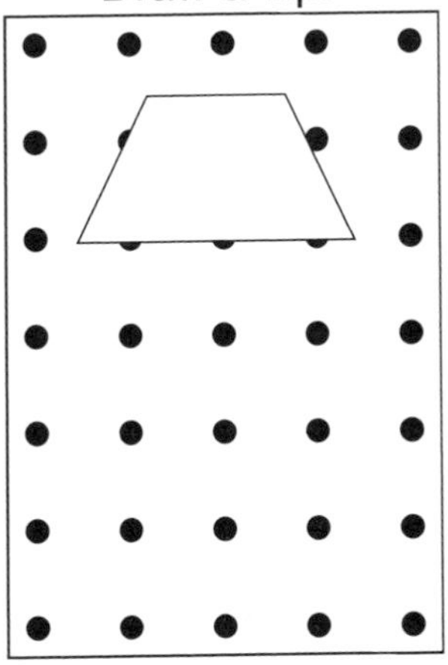

Draw a slide.

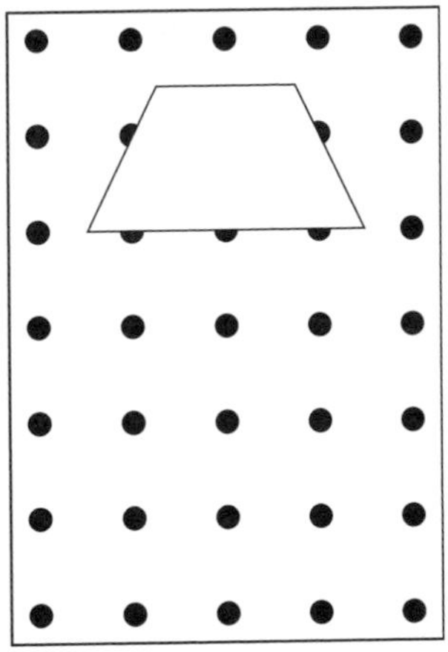

Draw a turn.

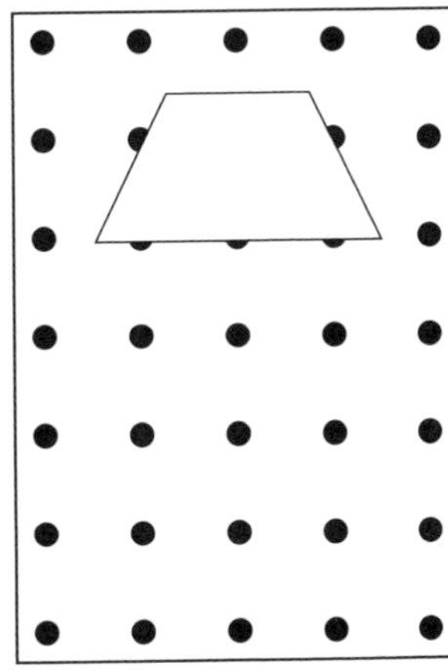

Draw a congruent figure to each figure already designed. Label whether it is a slide, turn, or flip.

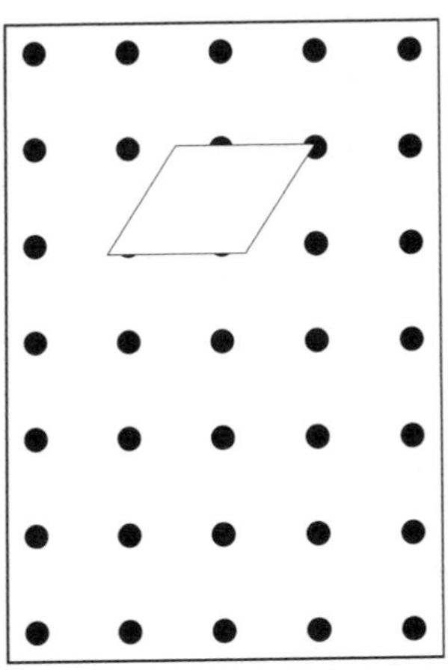

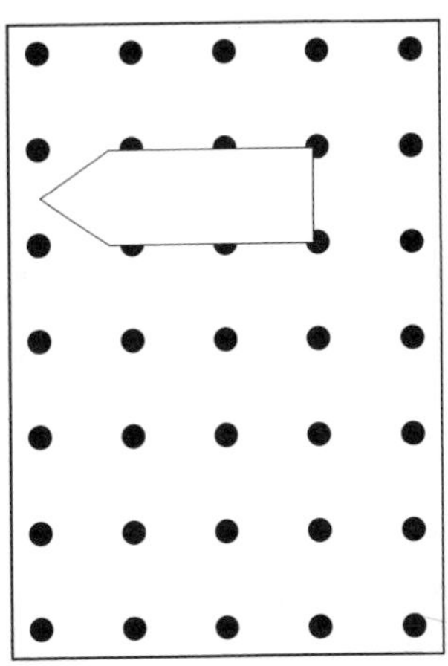

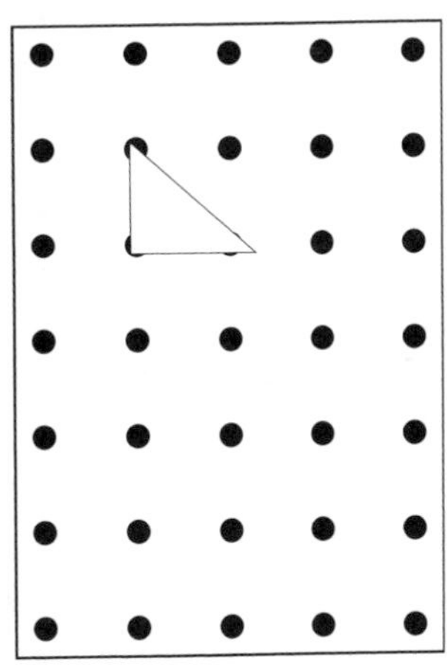

Congruent vs. Similar Shapes

Label which shapes are congruent and which are similar. **Congruent** shapes are the same shape and size. **Similar** shapes are the same shape but not necessarily the same size.

1.

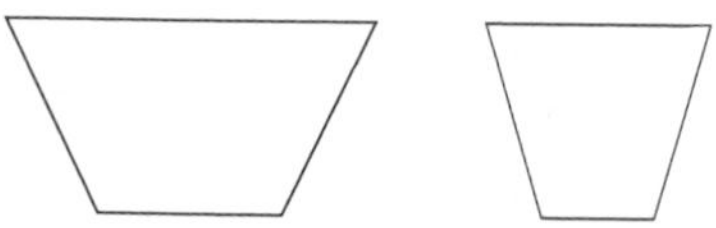

2.

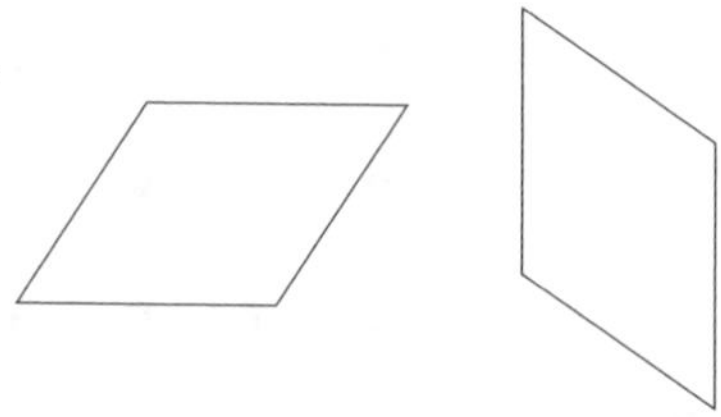

3.

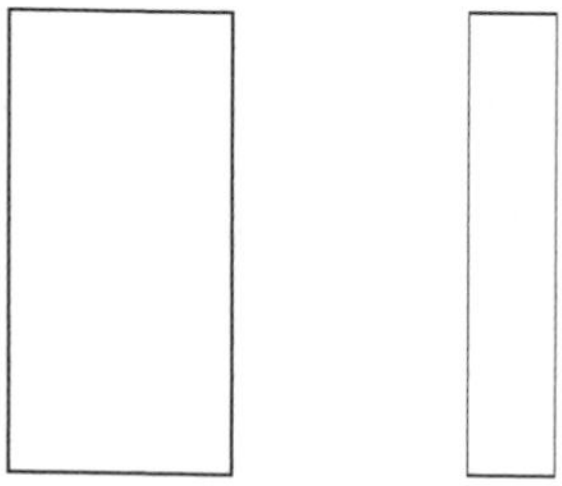

4.

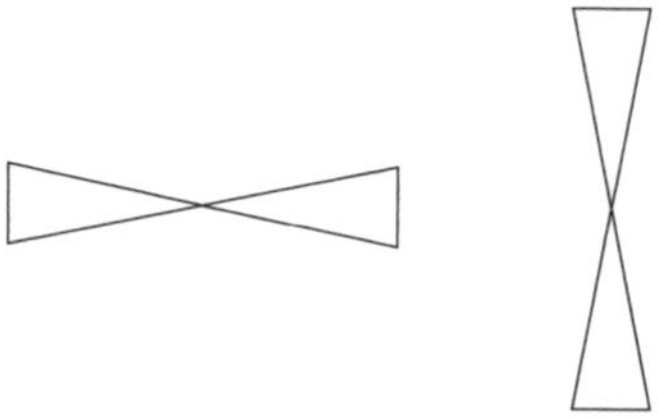

Draw a congruent shape.

5.

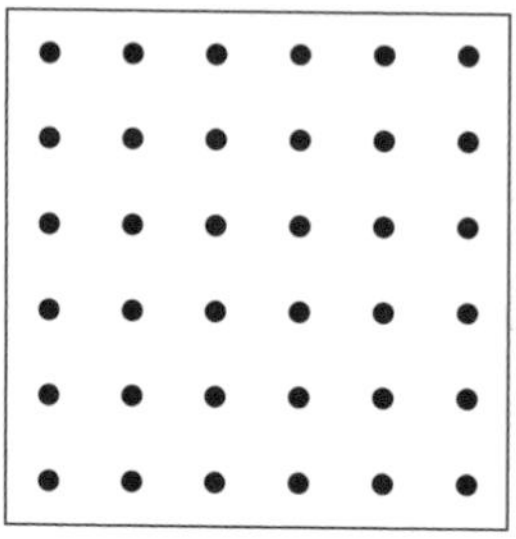

Draw a similar shape.

6.

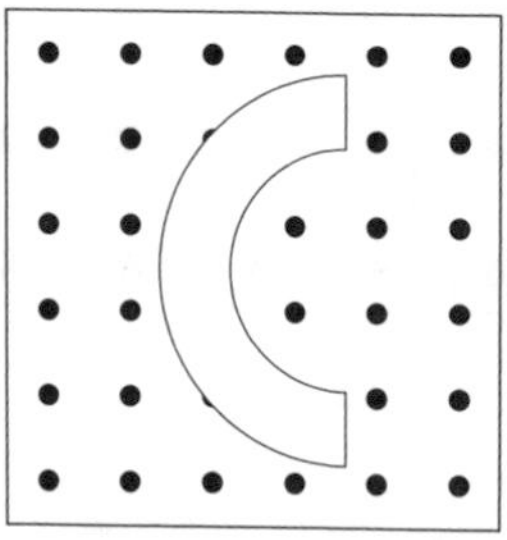

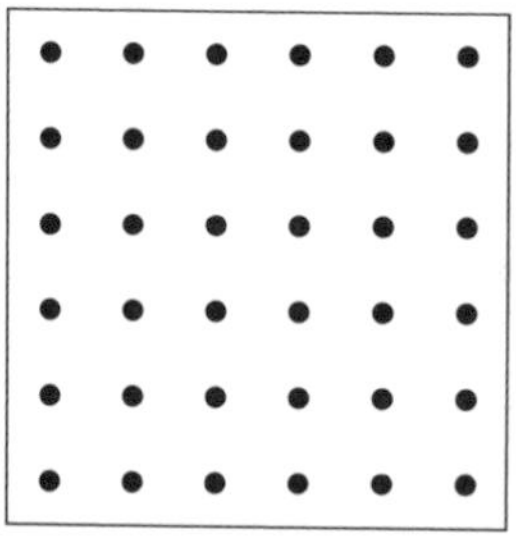

They're All around Us

Identify whether the images are a turn, slide, or flip. Write **turn**, **slide**, or **flip**.

Remember: A **turn** is when the figure rotates around a point. A **flip** is when the figure is flipped over a line. A **slide** is when the figure is moved along a straight line.

1. ________

2. ________

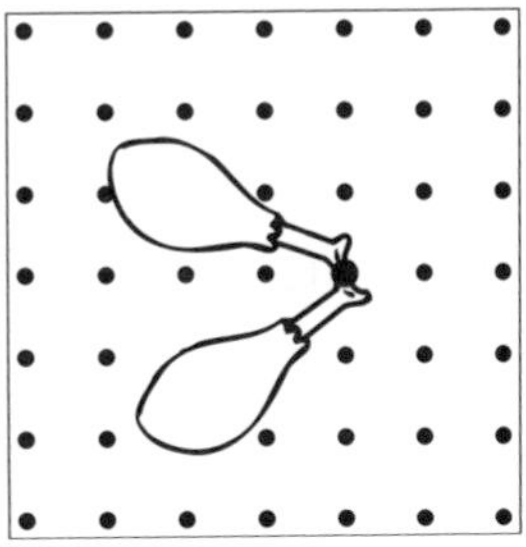

3. ________

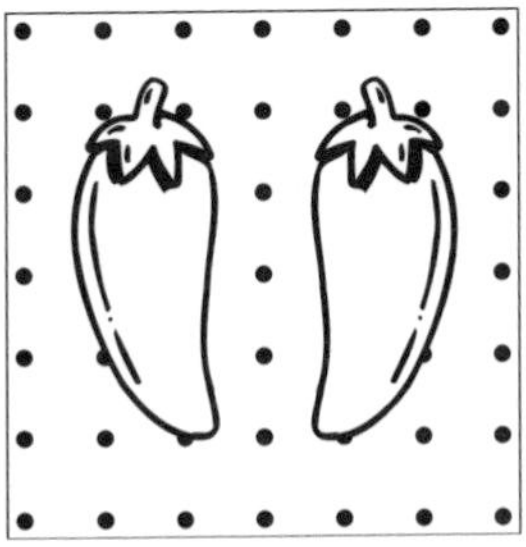

4. ________

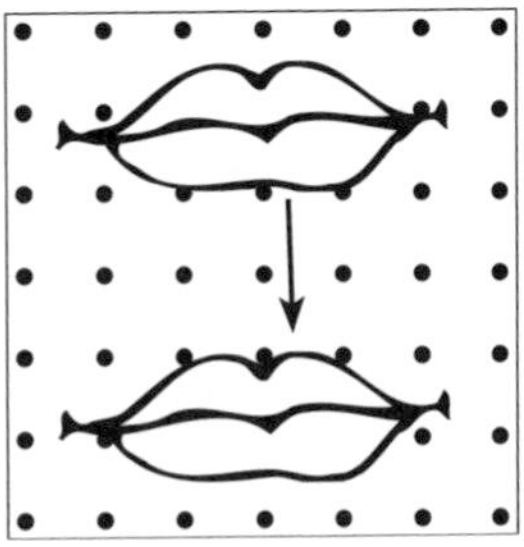

5. ________

6. ________

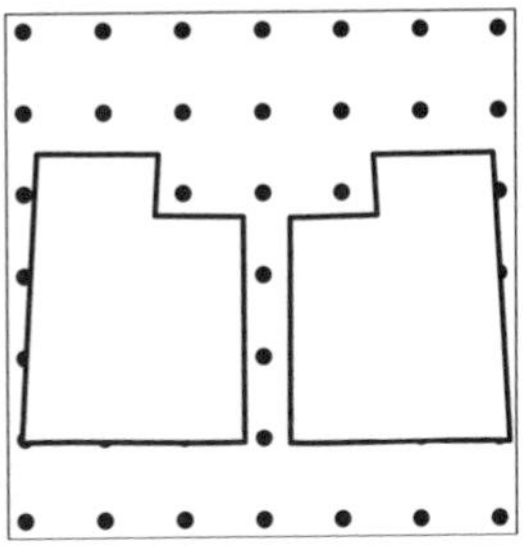

7. ________

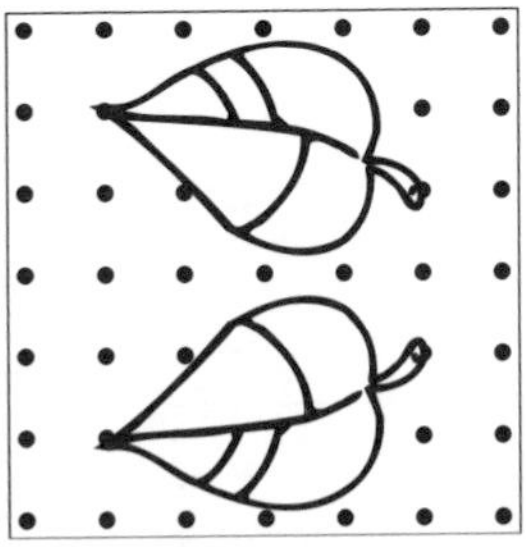

8. ________

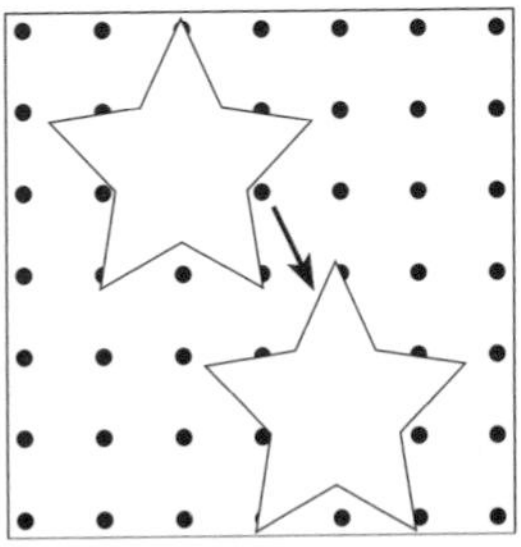

Turn Up the Volume!

Write the number of cubic units in each figure.

Remember: Volume tells the number of cubic units inside a figure.

1.

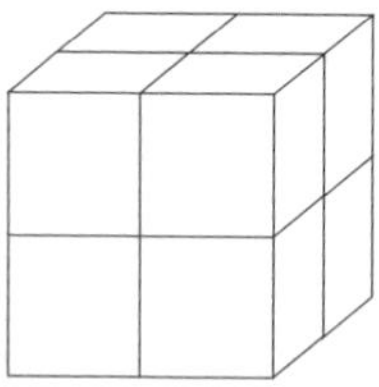

____________ cubic units

2.

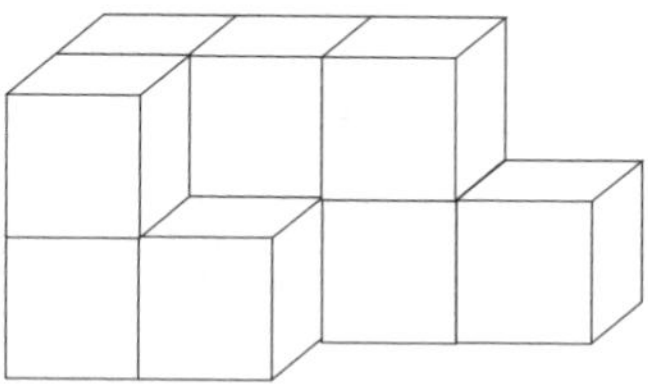

____________ cubic units

3.

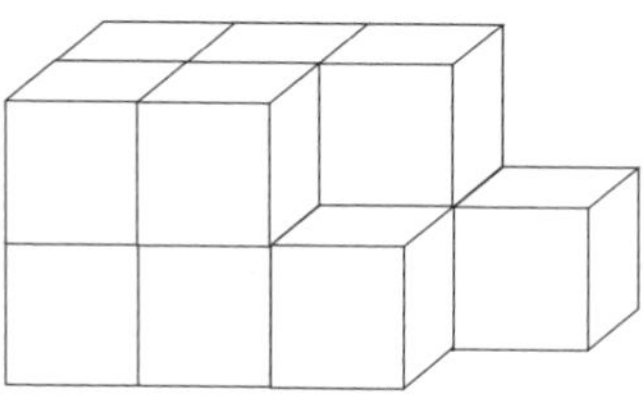

____________ cubic units

4.

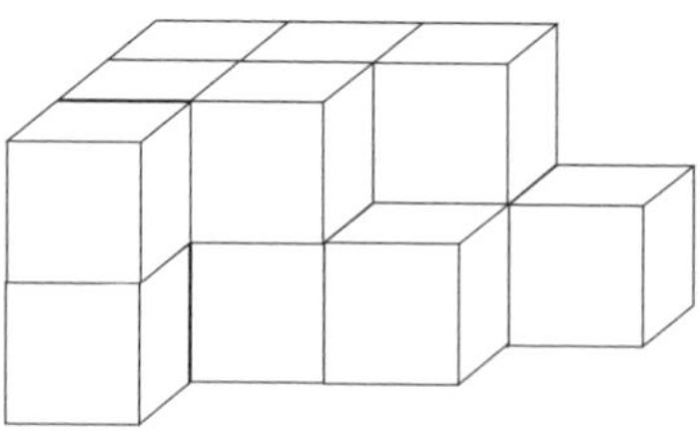

____________ cubic units

5.

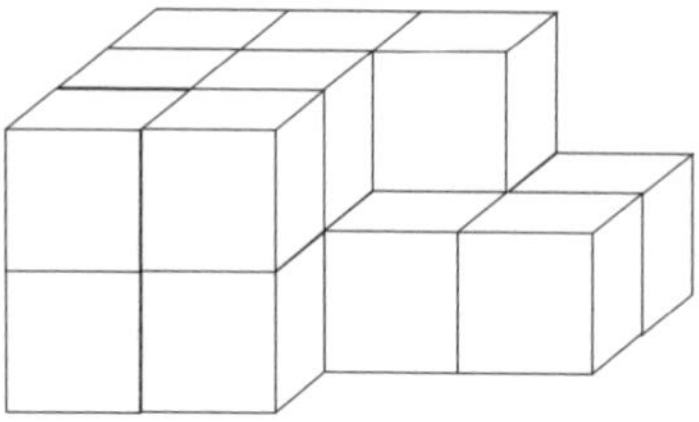

____________ cubic units

6.

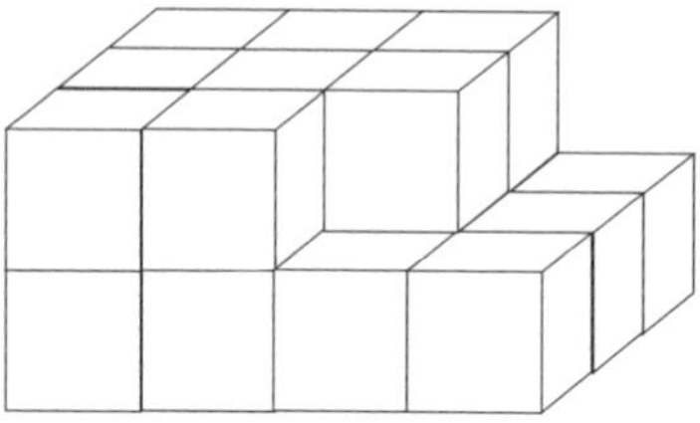

____________ cubic units

Finding the Volume

Use the mathematical formula to find the volume of each figure.

Example: **base x width x height = volume of a rectangular prism**

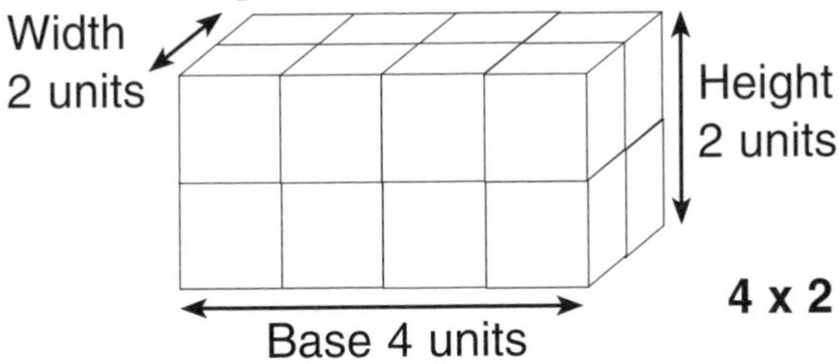

4 x 2 x 2 = __16__ cubic units

1.

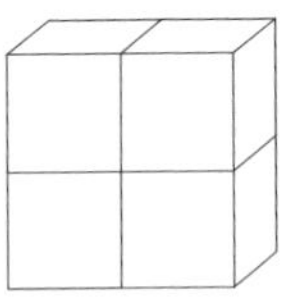

___ x ___ x ___ = ______

2.

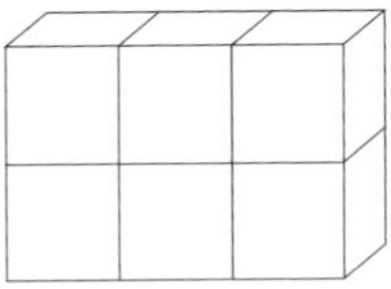

___ x ___ x ___ = ______

3.

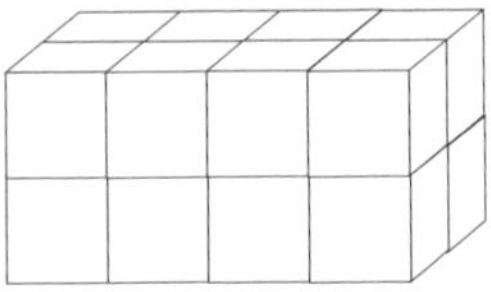

___ x ___ x ___ = ______

4.

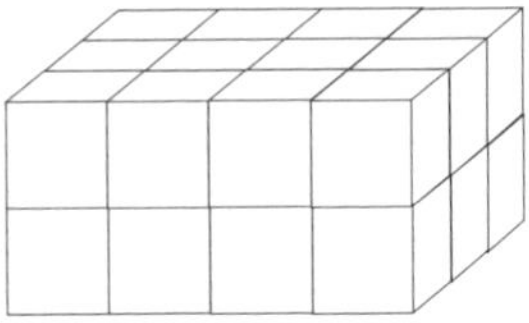

___ x ___ x ___ = ______

5.

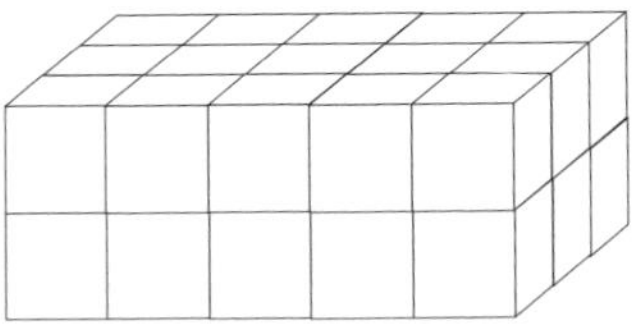

___ x ___ x ___ = ______

6.

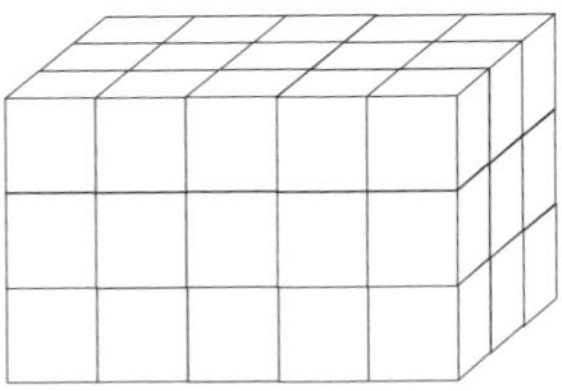

___ x ___ x ___ = ______

How Much Volume Is in a Rectangular Prism?

Complete the table.

	Length x	Width x	Height =	Volume
1.	6 mm	5 mm	2 mm	
2.	3 ft.	2 ft.	4 ft.	
3.	10 yd.	3 yd.	7 yd.	
4.	6 cm	8 cm	9 cm	

Draw and label each rectangular prism from the table above.

5. (prism #1)

6. (prism #2)

7. (prism #3)

8. (prism #4)

Pump Up the Volume

Find the volume of the figures below.

Remember: Volume = **l x w x h**

1.

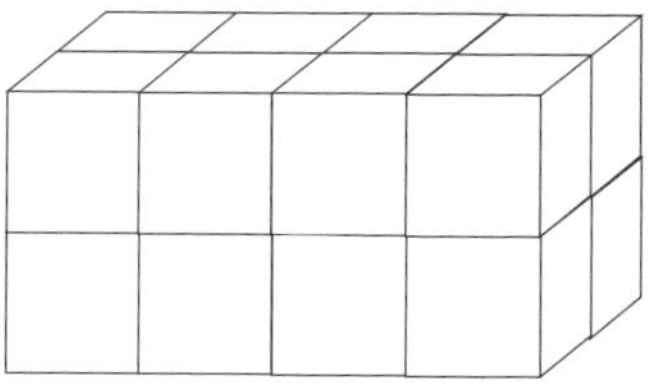

_____________ cubic units

2.

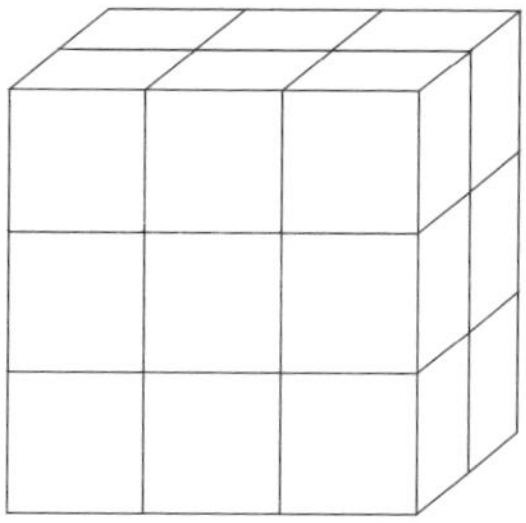

_____________ cubic units

3.

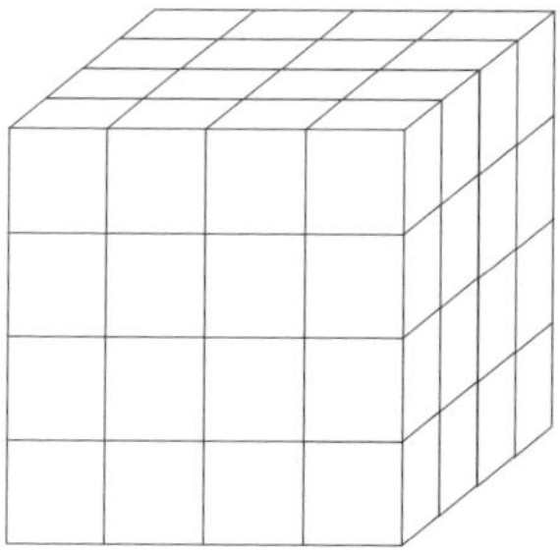

_____________ cubic units

4.

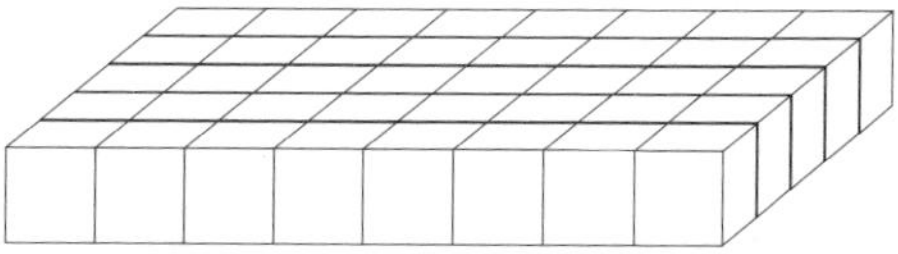

_____________ cubic units

5.

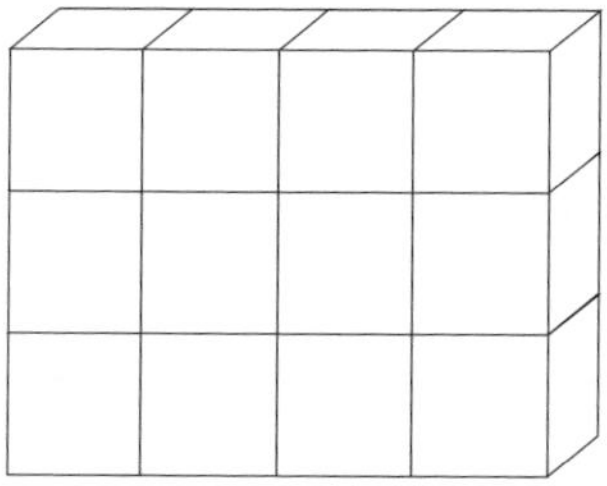

_____________ cubic units

6. Hint: Don't forget to subtract the middle area.

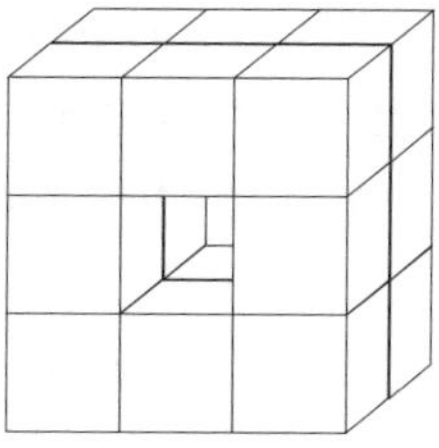

_____________ cubic units

Finding Volume Using Word Problems

Show your work in the box to the right of each word problem.

1. A toy box measures 24 in. x 18 in. x 36 in. What is the volume of the toy box?

2. Dad was building a new sandbox. It measured 12 ft. x 1 ft. x 6 ft. How much sand does he need to buy to fill the sandbox?

3. The shed in the Petersons' yard is 6 yd. x 3 yd. x 5 yd. How much space is in the shed?

4. A new stove measures 18 in. x 20 in. x 36 in. The space for the stove in the kitchen is 5,550 cubic inches. Will the new stove fit? Explain your answer.

____

____

____

That's "*A-Cute*" Triangle!

Identify each angle and label it in the space.

Example:

Right Angle—angle that measures 90 degrees (the angle forms a square corner)

Acute Angle—angle that measures less than a right angle, or less than 90 degrees

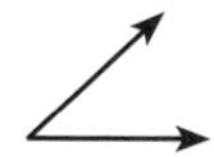

Obtuse Angle—angle that measures more than 90 degrees, or greater than a right angle

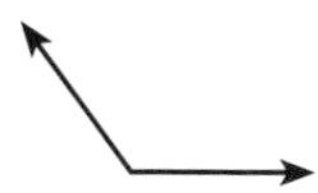

1.

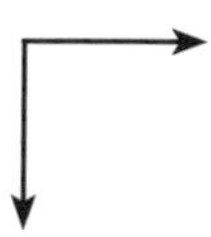

____

2.

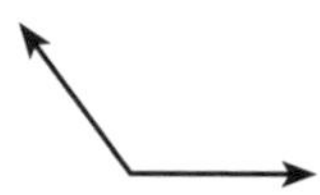

____

3.

____

4.

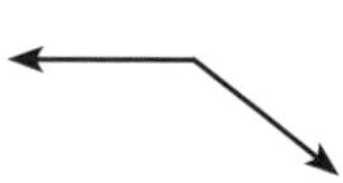

____

5.

____

6.

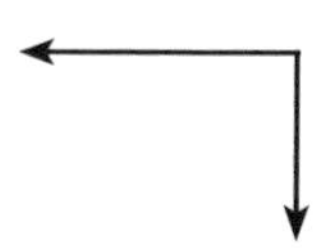

____

7.

____

8.

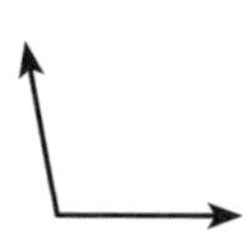

____

9.

____

Angles All Around

Label the following shapes according to the angles they contain. Write either **obtuse**, **right**, or **acute**. Some may have more than one answer.

1.

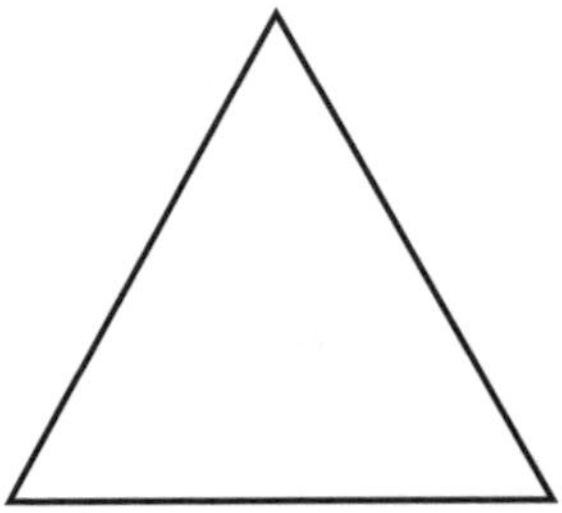

2.

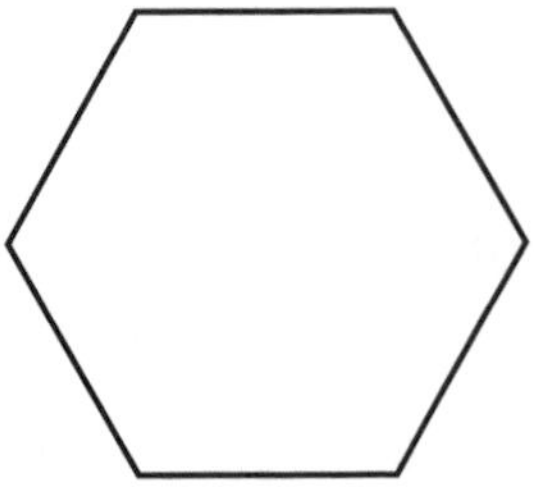

3.

4.

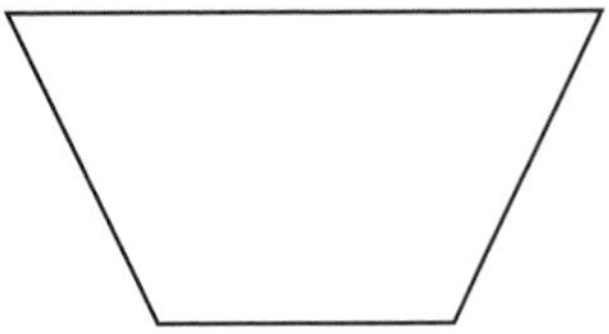

5.

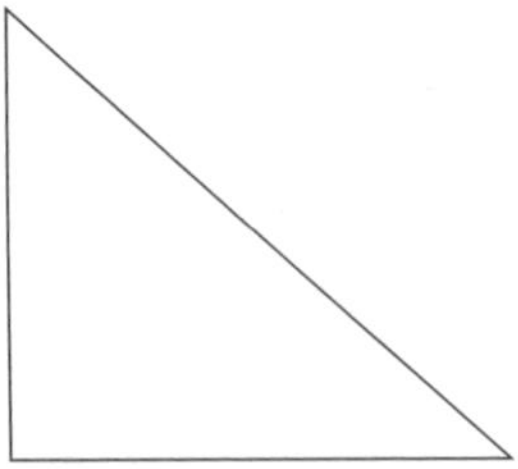

6.

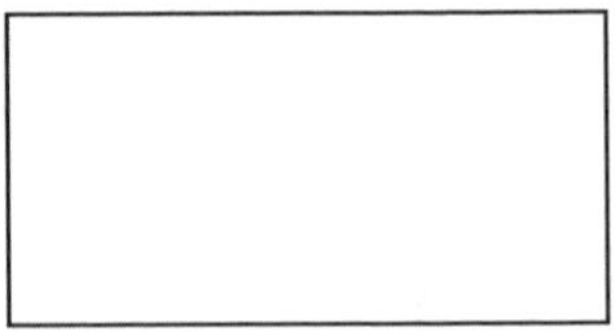

Label the Angles

Label the angle of each triangle. Write **acute**, **obtuse**, or **right**.

1.

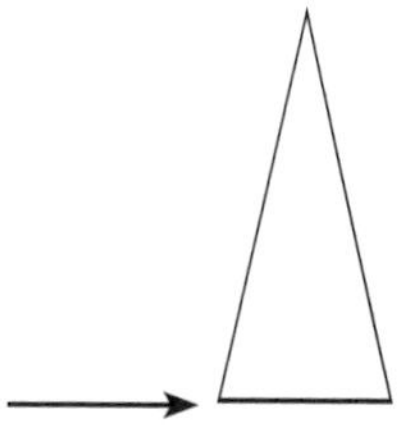

2.

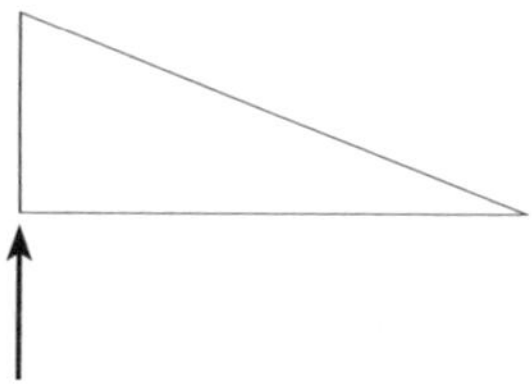

3.

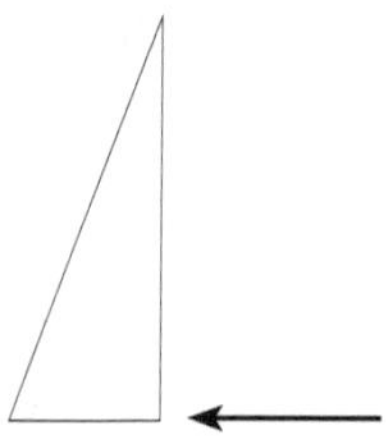

4.

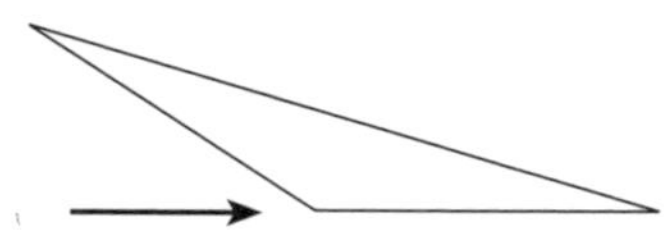

5.

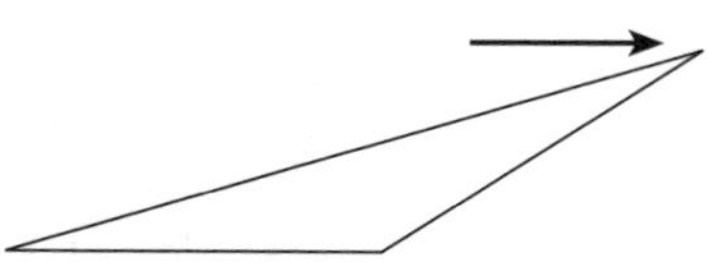

6.

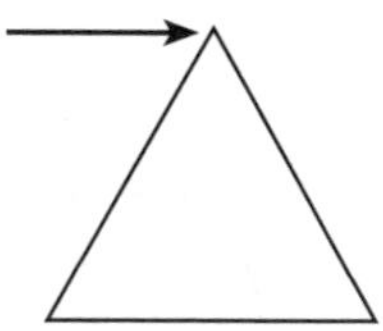

Angles

Label the following angles.

Example:

Obtuse

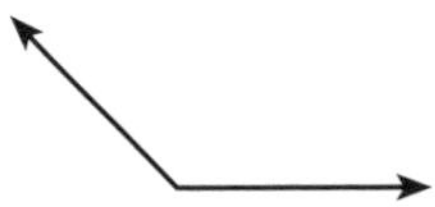

Right

Acute

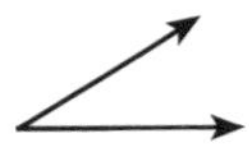

1.

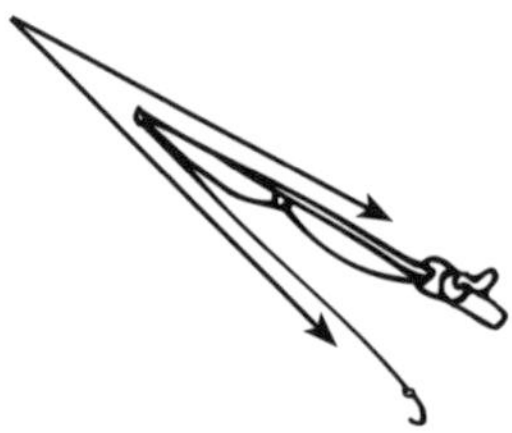

____

2.

____

3.

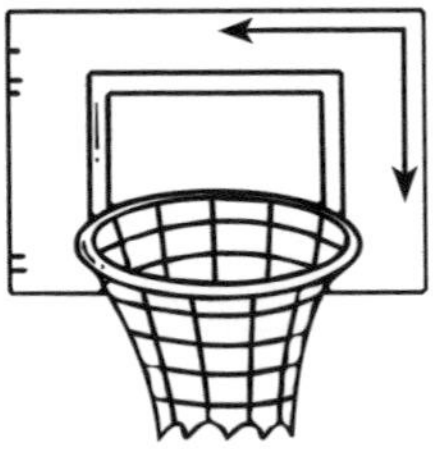

____

4.

____

5.

____

6.

____

Locate the Angle

Solve each problem.

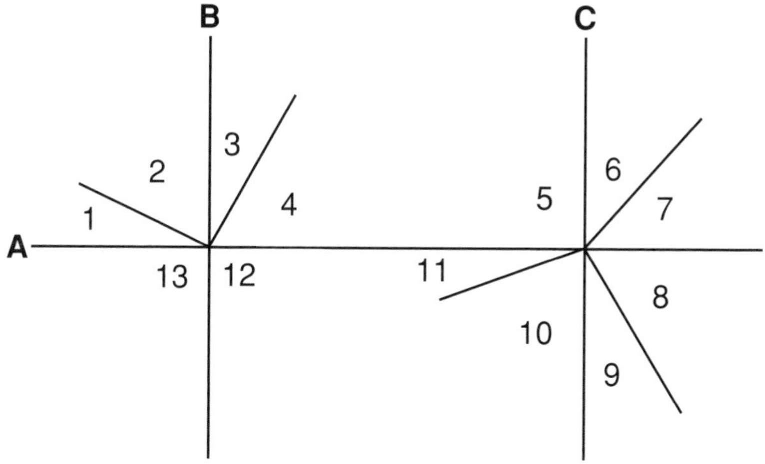

1. Name a pair of parallel lines. __________

2. Name four acute angles. ________________________

3. When combined, which pairs of angles form a right angle?

____

4. Name a pair of perpendicular lines. __________

5. Angle 10 is an __________ angle.

6. Angle 1 is an __________ angle.

7. Angle 8 is an __________ angle.

8. Line A is perpendicular to line __________.

9. Angles 8 and 9 make a __________ angle.

Reading and Writing Angles

Solve each problem.

Example:

Two rays with the same endpoint form an **angle**.

The endpoint is called the **vertex**.

Write the angle: ∠ XYZ
∠ ZYX
∠ Y

Read the angle: Angle XYZ
Angle ZYX
Angle Y

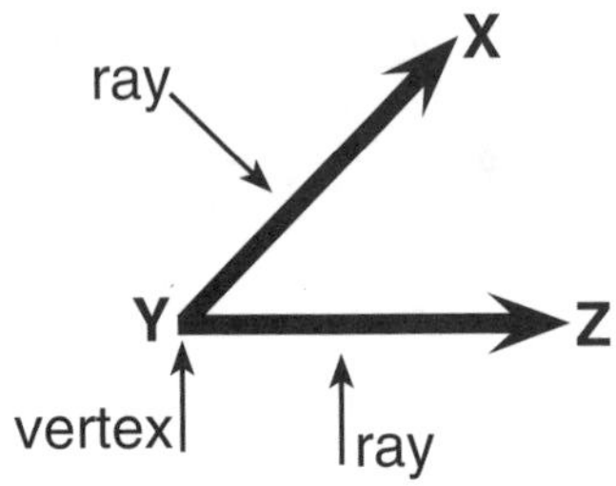

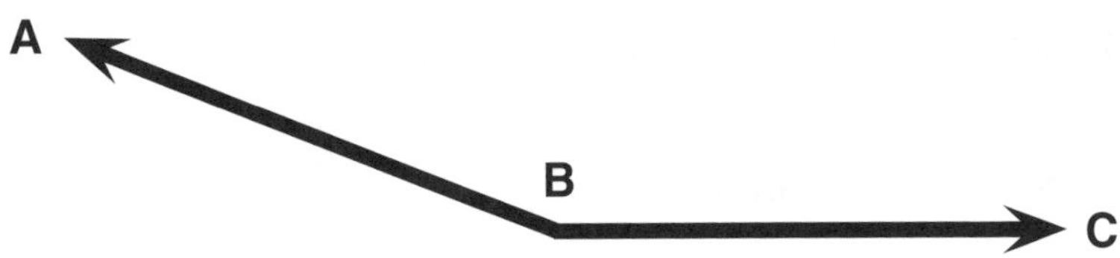

1. List two ways to write this angle. ______________________

2. Name the two rays. ______________________

3. Name the vertex. ______________________

4. What type of angle is this? ______________________

5. How do you read the angle using just one point on the angle?

____

6. The endpoint of two rays meet at what location? __________

Creating and Labeling Angles

Draw and label an example of the various parts of an angle.

1. ray XY	**2.** obtuse angle LMN
3. line segment PQ	**4.** right angle XYZ
5. point G	**6.** line ST
7. acute angle ABC	**8.** vertex P

Classifying Triangles

Equilateral Triangle—has three congruent sides
Isosceles Triangle—has only two congruent sides
Scalene Triangle—has no congruent sides

Classify the following triangles. Write **equilateral, isosceles**, or **scalene**.

1.

____

2.

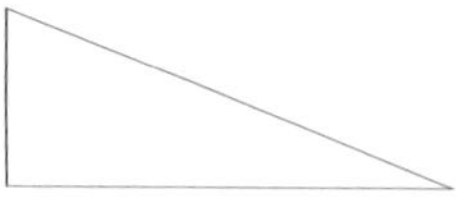

____

3.

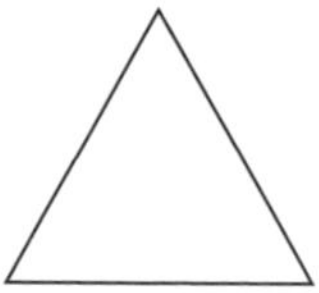

____

4.

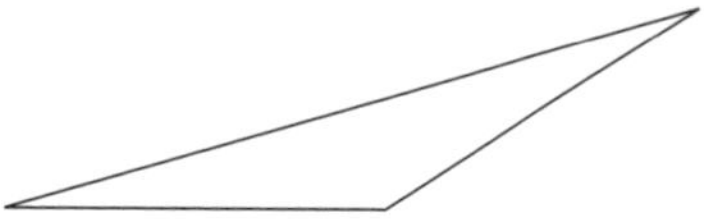

____

5.

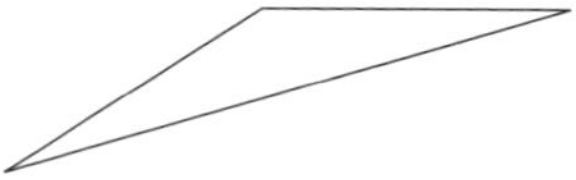

____

6.

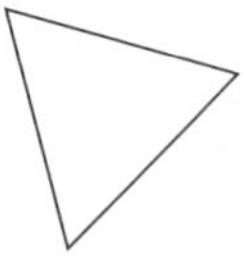

____

7.

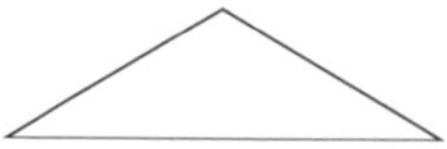

____

8.

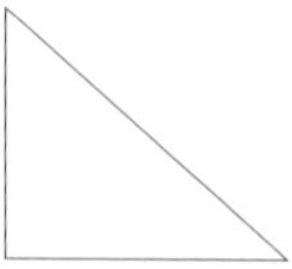

____

Identifying Triangles

Classify the triangle by the measurements given as **equilateral**, **isosceles**, or **scalene**. Draw the triangle and label it.

1. 23 mm, 23 mm, 23 mm

____

2. 19 ft., 6 ft., 15 ft.

____

3. 29 cm, 3 cm, 27 cm

____

4. 15 yd., 7 yd., 15 yd.

____

5. 17 in., 17 in., 17 in.

____

6. 9 mm, 9 mm, 4 mm

____

7. 76 cm, 70 cm, 76 cm

____

8. 29 yd., 28 yd., 6 yd.

____

Three-Dimensional Triangles

Finish the table.

Figure	Name	Number of Faces	Number of Edges	Number of Vertices
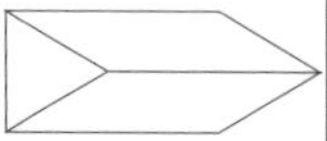	Triangular Prism			
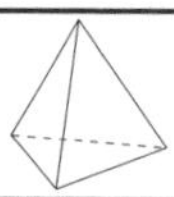	Triangular Pyramid			
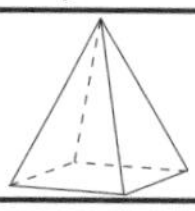	Square Pyramid			

Name the figures described below.

1. 9 edges ____________

2. 5 vertices ____________

3. 4 faces ____________

4. 6 vertices ____________

5. 4 vertices ____________

6. 8 edges ____________

7. 5 faces ____________

8. 6 edges ____________

Unknown Angles

Identify the unknown angle for each triangle. Use the space at the right to show your work.

Remember: The sum of the angles in a triangle is 180 degrees.

1.

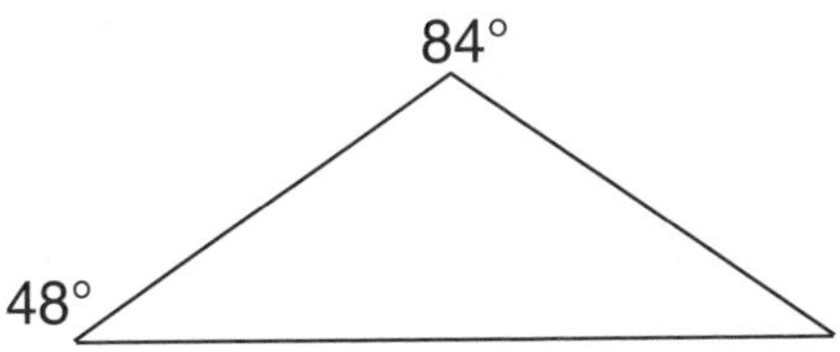

$$\begin{array}{r} \overset{1}{8}4 \\ +\ 48 \\ \hline 132 \end{array} \qquad \begin{array}{r} 1\overset{71}{\not{8}}0 \\ -\ 132 \\ \hline 48 \end{array}$$

missing angle = 48 degrees

2.

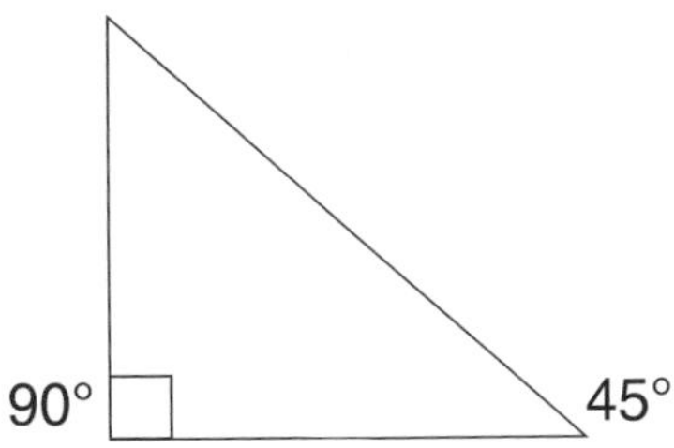

3.

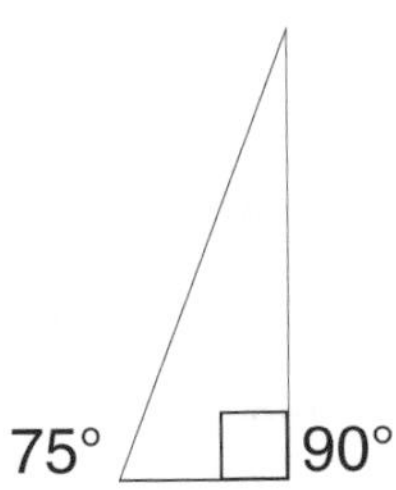

4.

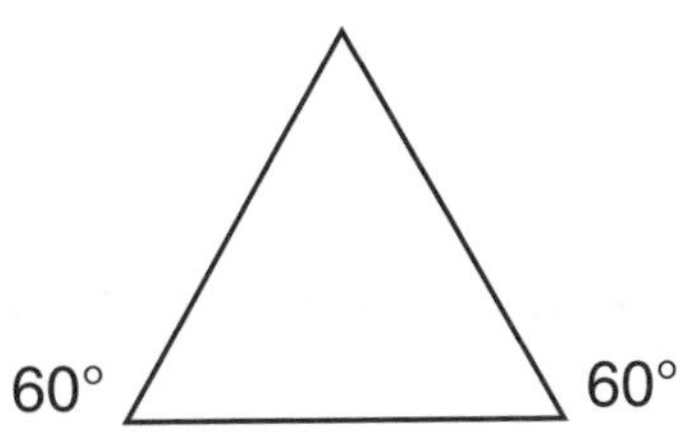

Word Problems—Angles and Triangles

Solve each problem. Write **scalene, isosceles, equilateral,** or **right.**

1. I have three sides and three angles. Only two angles are acute. What kinds of triangles could I be?

____

2. I am a triangle with two sides that have the same length. The angles opposite the equal sides are equal. What type of triangle am I?

____

3. I am a triangle with no angles the same and no sides the same length. What type of triangle am I?

____

4. I am a triangle with all three angles less than a right angle. What types of triangles could I be?

____

5. I am a triangle with all three sides equal and all three angles equal. What type of triangle am I?

____

6. I am a triangle with one angle larger than 90 degrees. What types of triangles could I be?

____

7. I am a triangle with one angle measuring 90 degrees. What type of triangle am I?

____

Find the Ordered Pair

Complete the ordered pair so that the missing number is two less than the second number. Then, graph each ordered pair.

Example:

(_____, 7) becomes (5, 7)

1. (_____, 10)

2. (_____, 5)

3. (_____, 9)

4. (_____, 3)

5. (_____, 6)

6. (_____, 8)

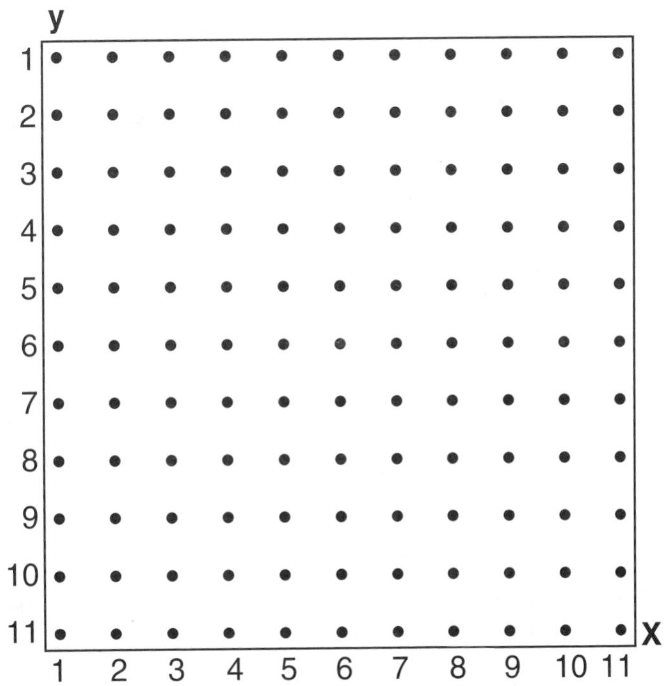

Find the Food

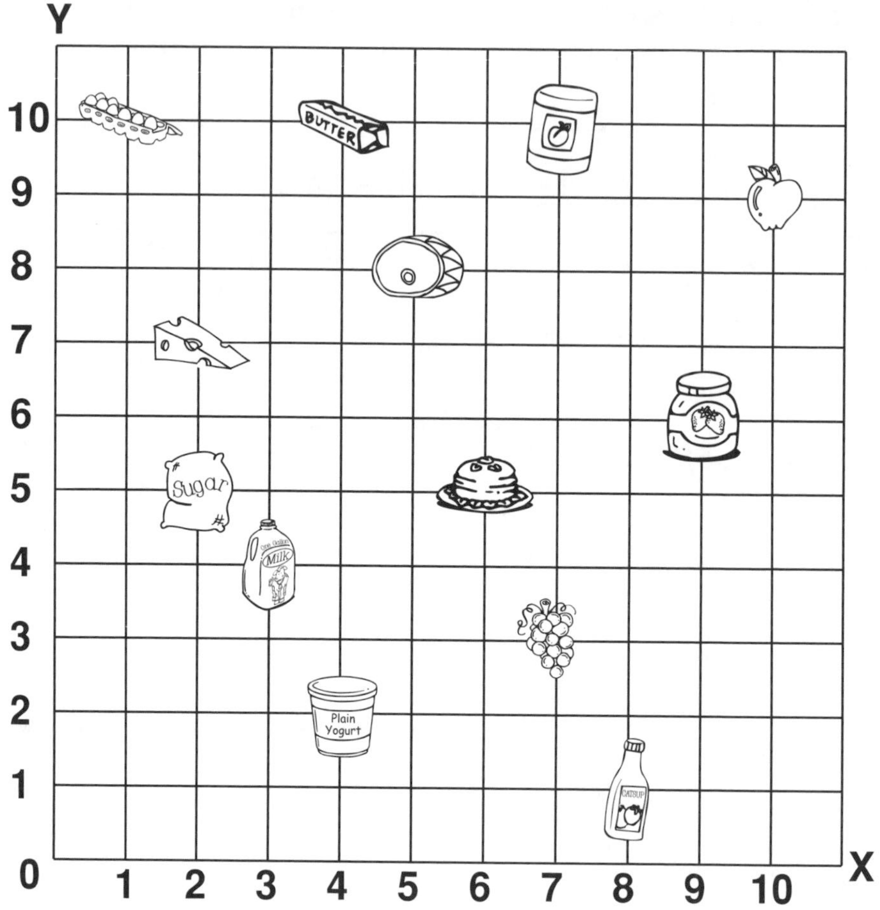

Given the ordered pairs listed below, locate the food in the grocery store. Remember to start at the x-axis first. Tell what food is at each coordinate.

x y

1. (7, 3) grapes ______ **2.** (2, 5) ______

3. (3, 4) ______ **4.** (1, 10) ______

5. (4, 2) ______ **6.** (10, 9) ______

7. (8, 1) ______ **8.** (5, 8) ______

9. (9, 6) ______ **10.** (2, 7) ______

Draw the Other Half

Plot each of the coordinate pairs; then, draw a line connecting the two coordinates. Connect all of the coordinate pairs in order to create half of an arrow. When you are finished, draw the mirror image of the left side of the arrow.

(E,1) ⟶ (D,1)

(D,1) ⟶ (C,1)

(C,1) ⟶ (C,2)

(C,2) ⟶ (C,3)

(C,3) ⟶ (C,4)

(C,4) ⟶ (C,5)

(C,5) ⟶ (C,6)

(C,6) ⟶ (C,7)

(C,7) ⟶ (B,7)

(B,7) ⟶ (A,7)

(A,7) ⟶ (B,8)

(B,8) ⟶ (C,9)

(C,9) ⟶ (D,10)

(D,10) ⟶ (E,11)

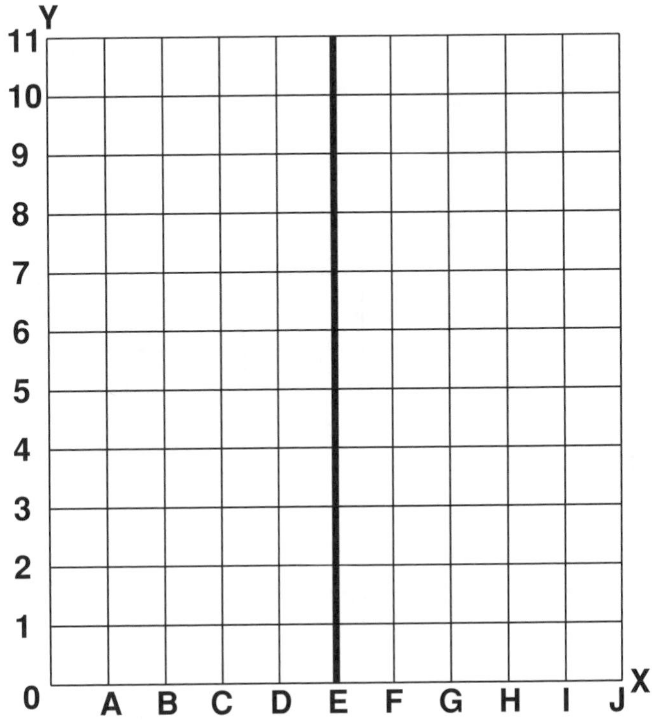

The Perfect Place

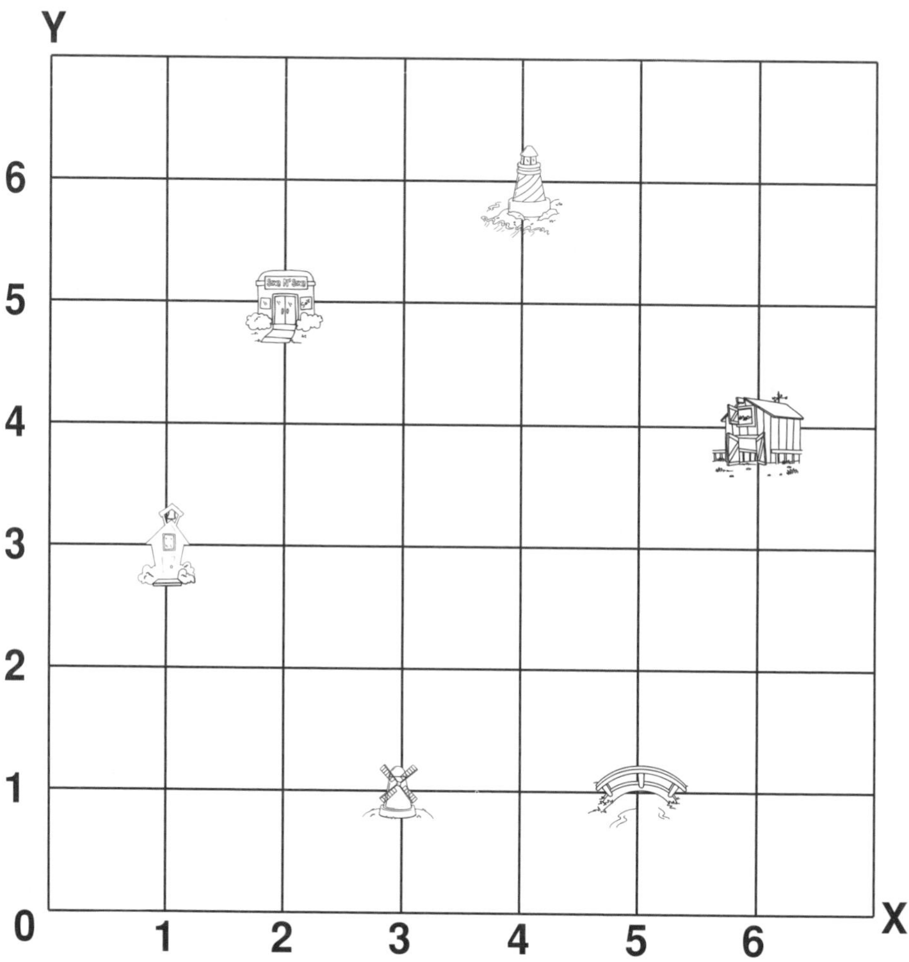

Locate the following places on your grid, and record the coordinates.

1. bridge (___x___, ___y___)
2. windmill (____, ____)
3. barn (____, ____)
4. school (____, ____)
5. grocery store (____, ____)
6. lighthouse (____, ____)

Sorting Shapes

Sort the following plane figures in the Venn diagram.

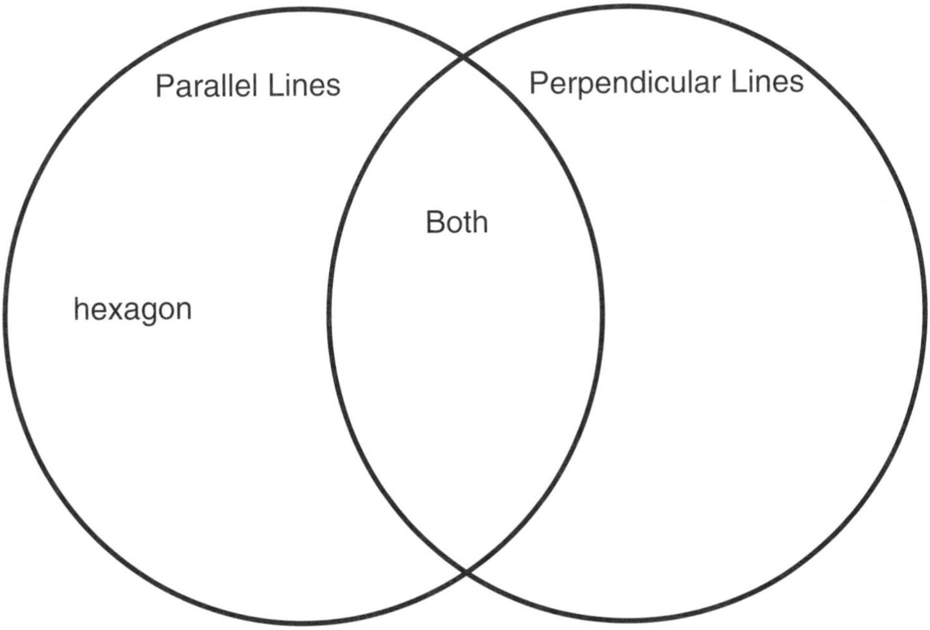

Word Bank

hexagon	parallelogram
rectangle	octagon
square	right triangle
pentagon	

Regular or Not?

Sort the following shapes into the circle they best fit.

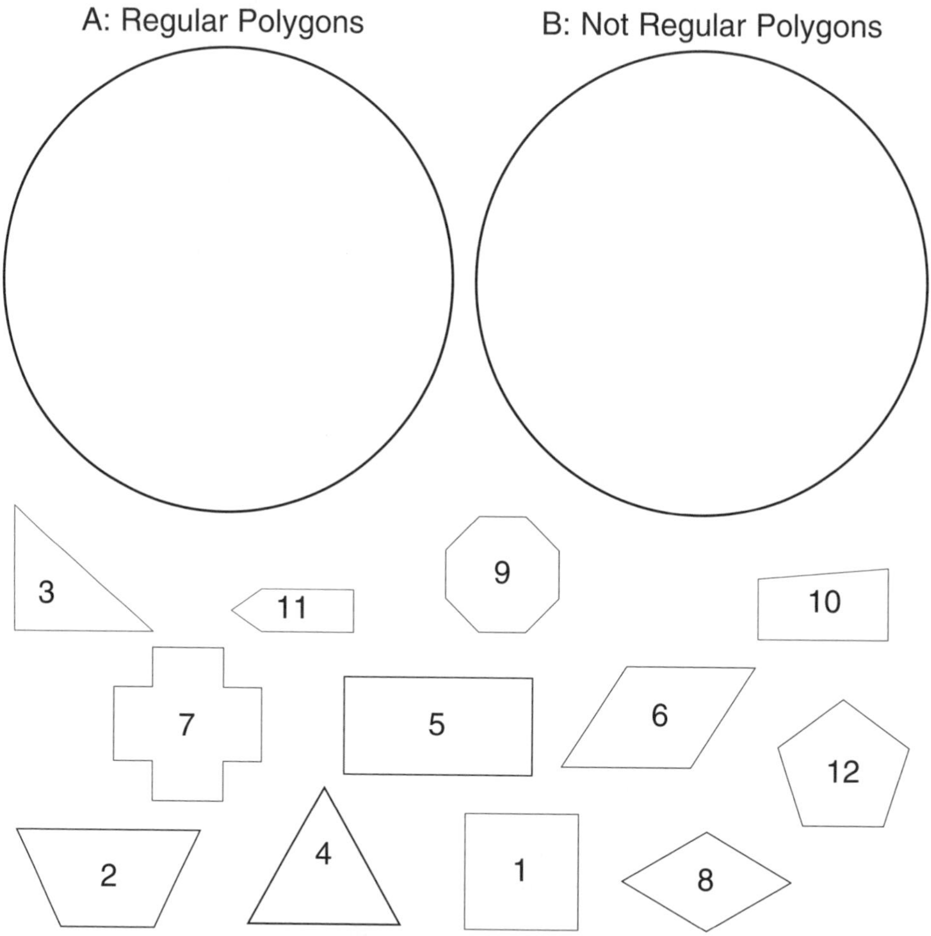

13. What best describes the shapes in circle A?

____

____

____

14. What best describes the shapes in circle B?

____

____

____

Just "Plane" Old Shapes

Sort the following shapes into the circle they best fit.

A: **With** Four or More Congruent Sides

B: **Without** Four Congruent Sides

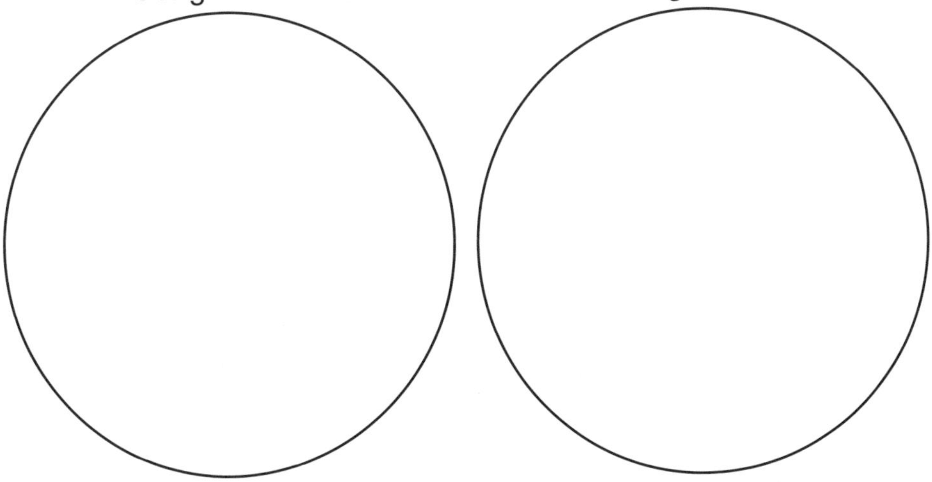

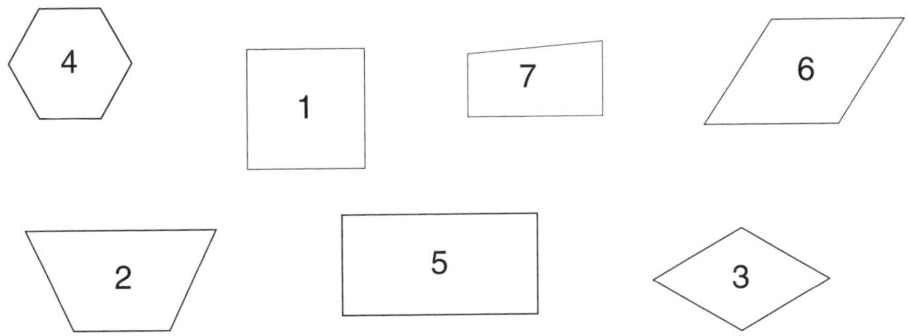

Use proper terminology to answer the following questions.

8. What best describes the shapes in circle A?

____

____

____

9. What best describes the shapes in circle B?

____

____

____

Triangle Venn Diagram

Describe how acute angles and equilateral triangles are related in this Venn diagram.

Remember: An **equilateral triangle** has three congruent sides.

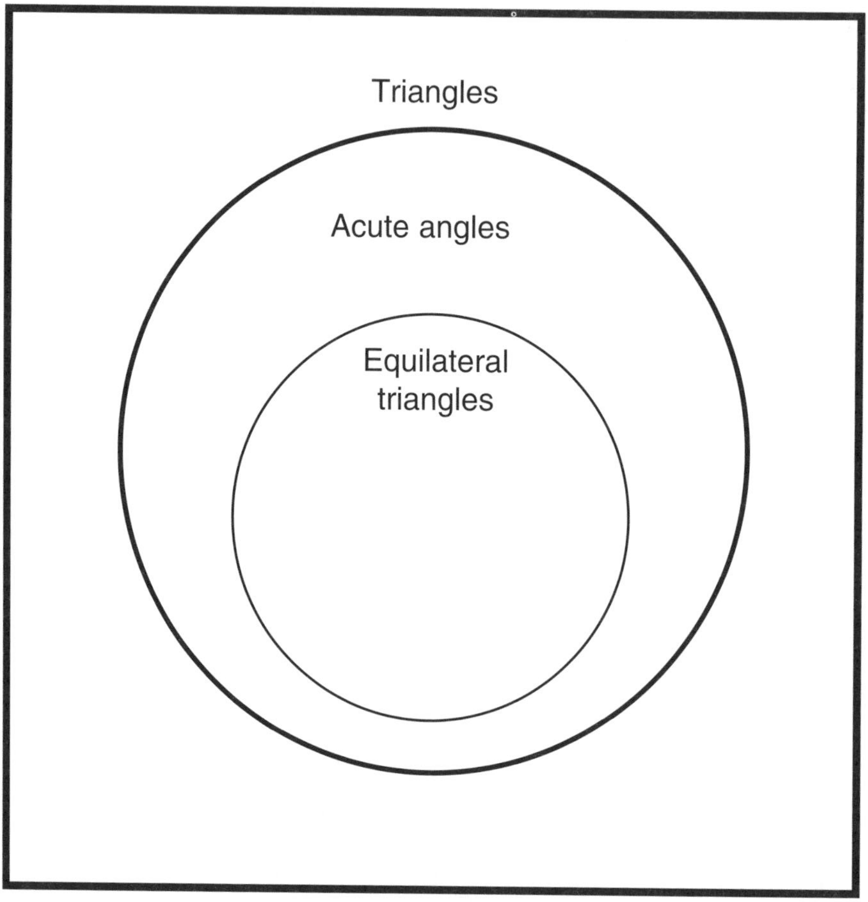

All around the Town

First, on the grid draw in the following places at the coordinates listed below.

bus stop (8,2) mail box (10,3) swimming pool (5,7)

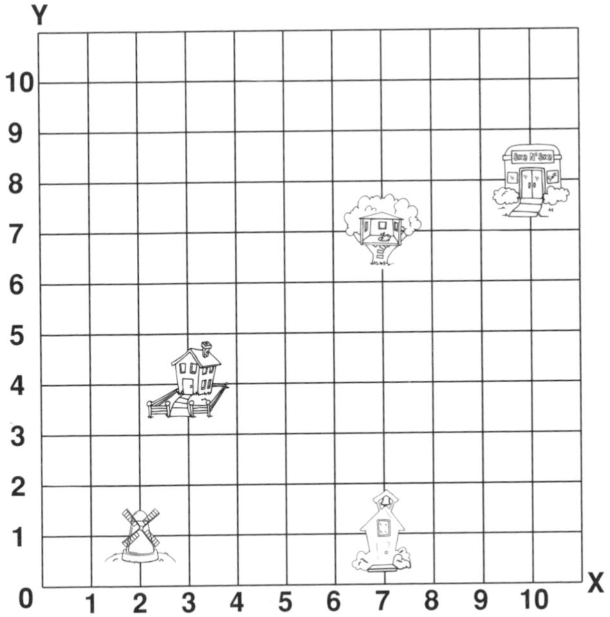

Then, answer the following questions.

1. If you start at (2,1) and go to (10,8), at what places did you start and stop? ________________ and ________________

2. What are the coordinates for the park?____________________

3. When you leave school, you are at what coordinates? ______ Then, you go to (8,2), which is the ________________, and it takes you to the tree house which is at __________.

4. The house is at what coordinates? ________________________

5. Your mom had you do an errand before you could go swimming. She sent you to (10,3). Where did your mom need you to go? ________________________

6. Your two favorite places are the tree house and the swimming pool. What are their coordinates? ______ and _______

Coordinate Geometry Riddle

Identify the letter for each ordered pair listed in the answer. This will help you to answer the riddle below.

Riddle: What is the lowest point in the United States?

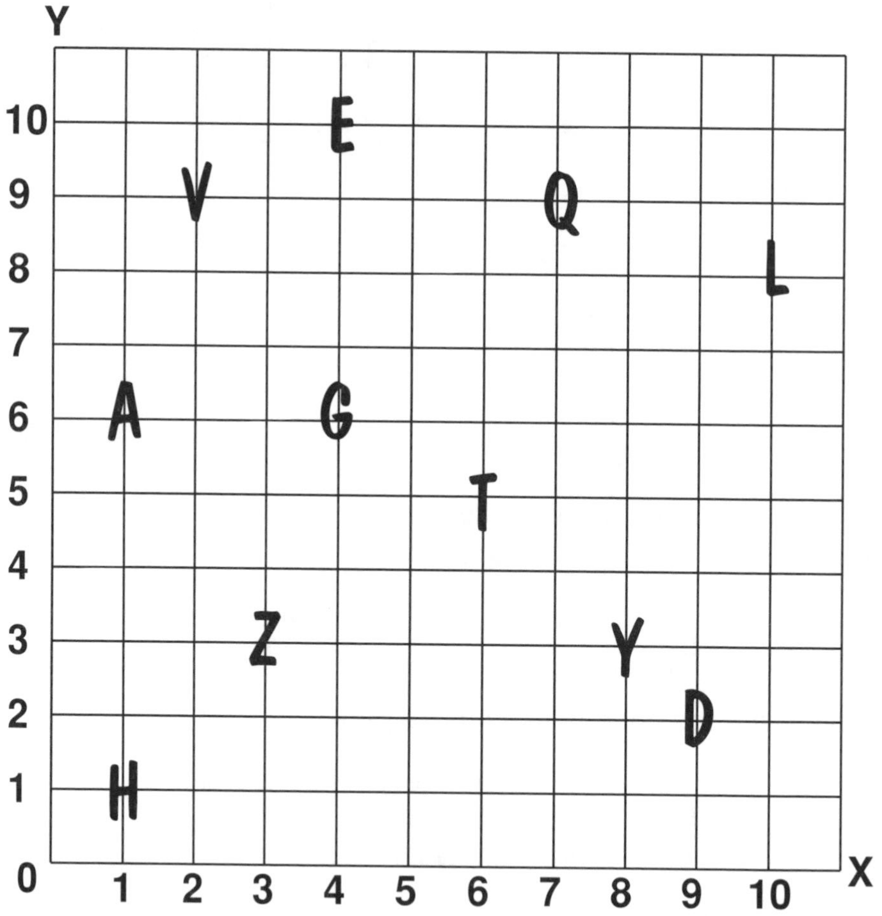

Answer:

____ ____ ____ ____ ____   ____ ____ ____ ____ ____ ____

(9,2) (4,10) (1,6) (6,5) (1,1)   (2,9) (1,6) (10,8)(10,8)(4,10)(8,3)

Draw the Object

Draw a specific object using the directions and the shapes. You may change the size or rotate the shape as needed.

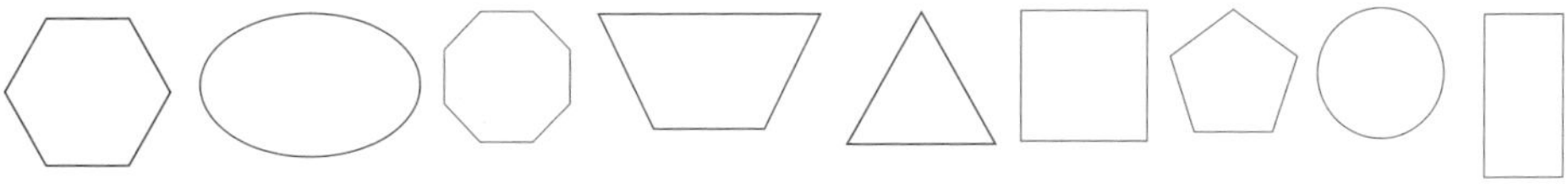

Example:

Draw a tree using 3 triangles and 1 rectangle.

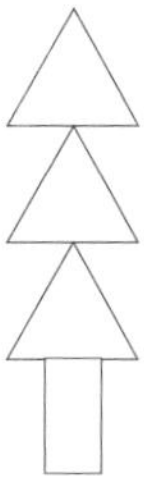

Draw an ice cream cone using 1 triangle and 3 circles.	
Draw a train using 1 triangle, 1 rectangle, and 3 circles.	
Draw a house using 1 pentagon, 1 rectangle, 2 squares, and 1 circle.	
Draw a robot using 1 octagon, 3 ovals, 4 rectangles, and 1 square.	
Draw flowers in a pot using 1 trapezoid, 3 rectangles, 3 hexagons, and 18 ovals.	

Critical Thinking Skills

You Be the Teacher

Solve each problem.

1. Marty said that he drew a triangle with two right angles Describe and correct the error.

____

____

____

____

2. The radius of Kyle's circle is 18 in. The diameter of Tyler's circle is 36 in. Tyler says his circle is bigger. Describe and correct his error.

____

____

____

____

3. Katelyn said all angles in an octagon are acute. Describe and correct her error.

____

____

____

____

Polygons

Find four different ways to make a polygon that touches four dots, but has NO dots inside. Be sure each polygon is different (not congruent).

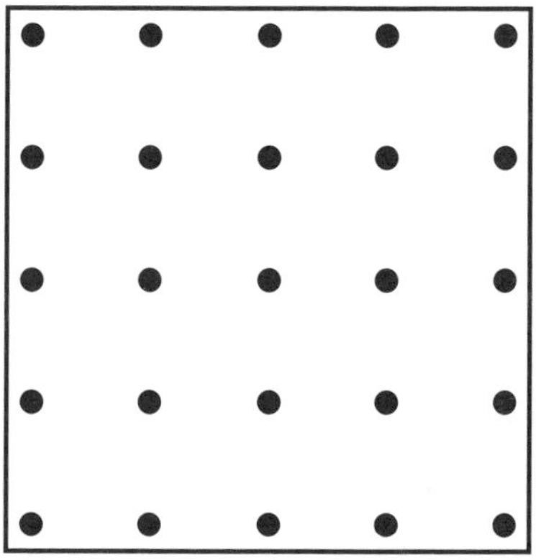

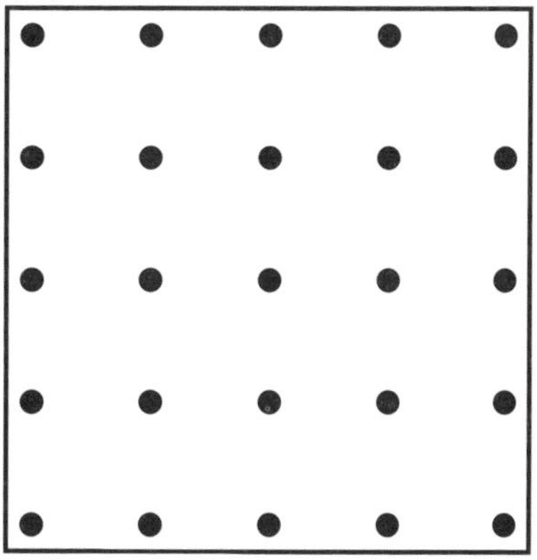

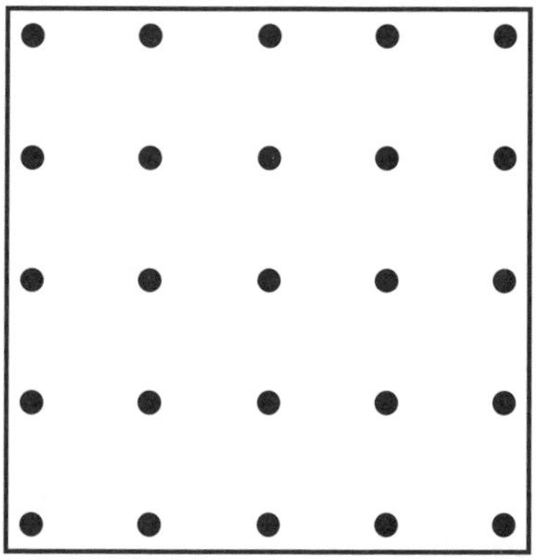

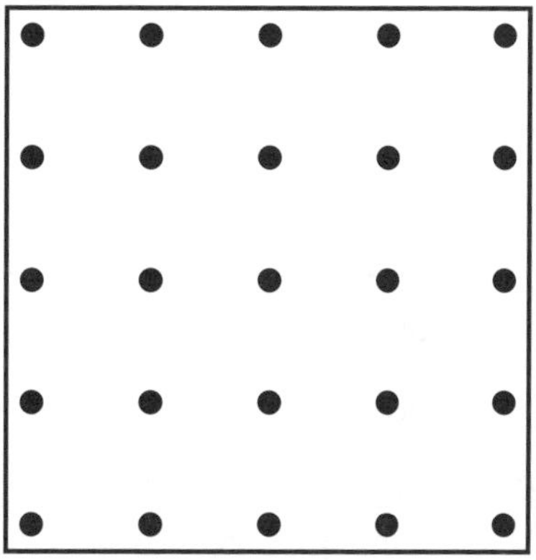

Word Search

Use the shape definitions at the bottom to find the name of the shapes in the word search.

s	l	h	j	r	x	x	q	y	h	d	q	w	c
n	i	u	e	e	n	d	o	t	r	o	u	x	t
o	o	l	l	c	o	n	g	s	b	p	a	t	o
g	s	r	g	t	g	o	b	q	s	j	d	j	z
a	e	q	n	a	y	g	y	u	u	c	r	f	m
x	c	c	a	n	l	a	q	a	w	x	i	y	w
e	v	f	i	g	o	t	g	r	a	g	l	u	f
h	f	f	r	l	p	n	c	e	i	f	a	w	e
h	h	g	t	e	g	e	r	o	n	v	t	r	z
i	x	e	m	a	c	p	n	h	l	m	e	b	k
z	r	t	r	a	p	e	z	o	i	d	r	l	x
a	z	z	y	f	v	m	v	h	f	u	a	w	h
z	k	d	p	k	t	c	t	h	w	i	l	t	i
l	p	q	e	v	i	n	h	y	z	v	s	v	j

a polygon with six sides and six angles

a polygon with three angles

a plane figure in which all angles are right angles; opposite sides are parallel, and opposite angles are equal

a five-sided polygon

a rectangle with all four sides equal

three or more line segments connected so that an area is enclosed inside

four-sided figures

a quadrilateral with two sides not parallel and two sides parallel

Space Figures

Critical Thinking Skills

Write the names of the following figures.

1. 

____

2. 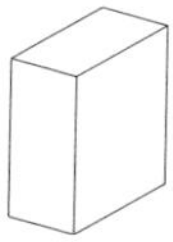

____

3. 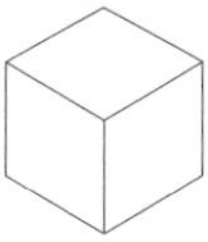

____

4. 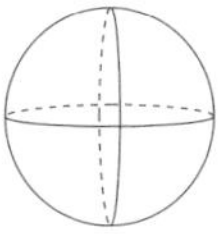

____

5. 

____

Describe the figure below using geometric vocabulary (like *vertex, face, edge, sphere, cylinder, cube, cone, square pyramid*).

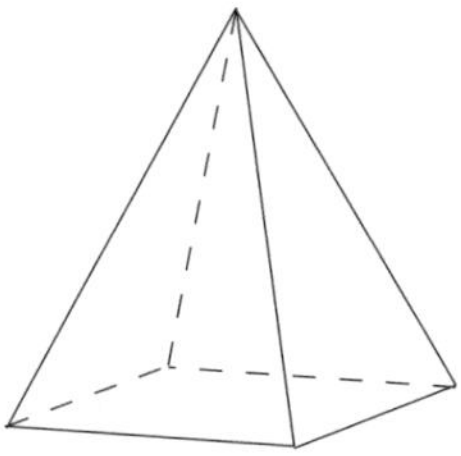

6. ______________________

____

____

____

Look at the shapes on side A and side B. Write two things you notice about the shapes on side A compared to side B.

7. ______________________

____

8. ______________________

____

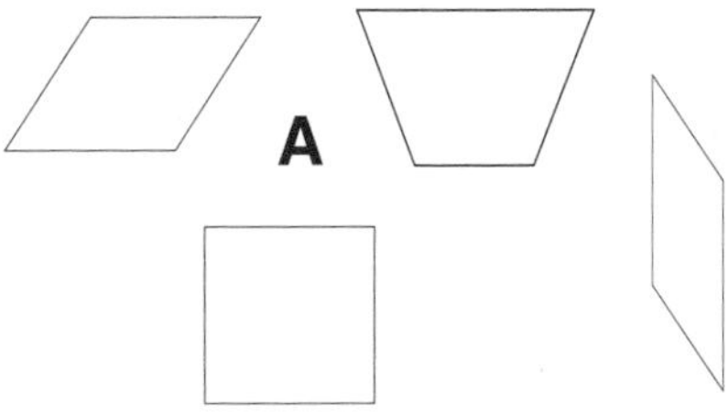

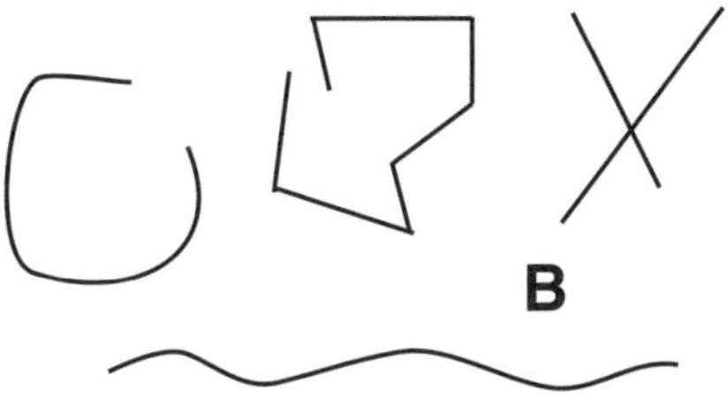

Classroom Shapes

Find and circle these shapes in the picture below:
16 squares, 4 rectangles, 21 circles, 4 triangles,
2 pentagons, 2 trapezoids

Lines and Shapes Crossword Puzzle

Across

1. It has three sides and three angles.

3. It is made up of three or more line segments connected so that the area is closed in.

5. They always have four sides.

8. It has four sides. Opposite angles are the same size.

Down

2. It has pairs of opposite sides that are parallel, and all sides are congruent.

4. It has four equal sides and four right angles.

6. It has four right angles and two pairs of equal sides, each pair a different length.

7. It has one pair of opposite sides that are parallel but not equal.

Puzzling Pieces

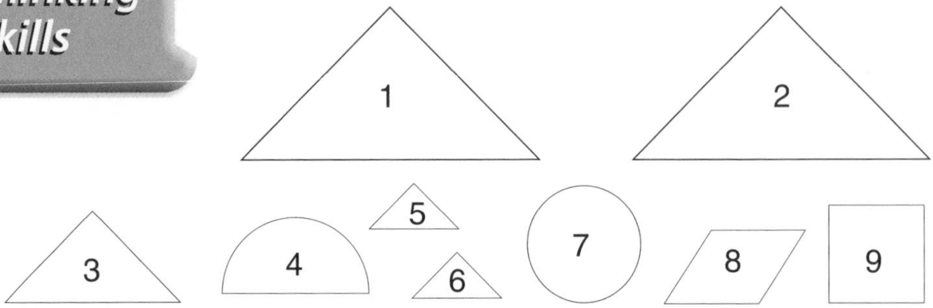

1. Identify which of the shapes above will form a square when put together.

____

2. Which shapes would not fit in the square? Explain why.

____

____

____

3. What do you call this Chinese puzzle where seven shapes put together form a square?

____

____

Answer Pages

Page 1
1. D 2. A 3. E 4. F 5. I
6. C 7. G 8. B

Page 2
A. 8 B. 3 C. 1 D. 9 E. 6
F. 2 G. 5 H. 4 I. 7

Page 3
A. 4 B. 2 C. 7 D. 5 E. 3
F. 1 G. 10 H. 6 I. 9 J. 8

Page 4
A. 4 B. 2 C. 5
D. 1 E.3 F. 6

Page 5
1. cube

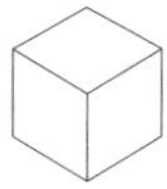

2. cylinder

3. sphere

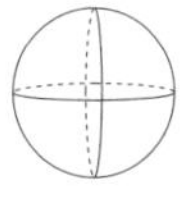

4. cone

5. rectangular prism

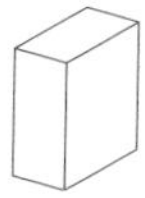

6. triangular pyramid

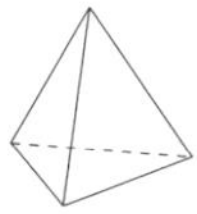

Page 6
A. 1 B. 3 C. 2 D. 6
E. 4 F. 5 G. 8 H. 7

Page 7

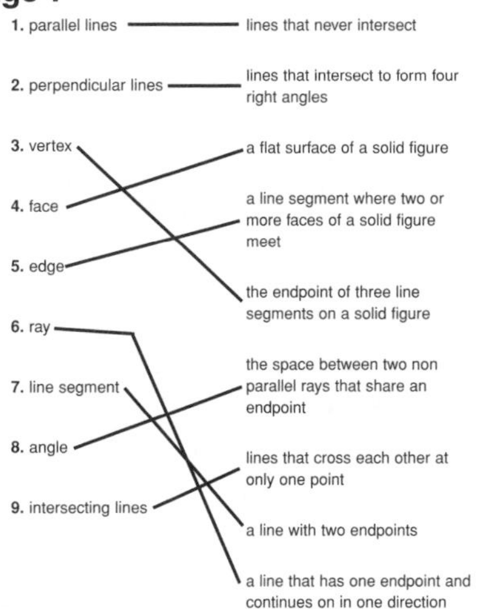

Page 8
1. regular 2. regular
3. not regular 4. not regular
5. not regular 6. regular
7. regular 8. not regular

Page 9

This triangle has three sides.

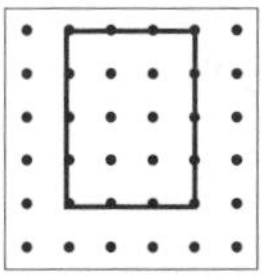

This quadrilateral has four sides.

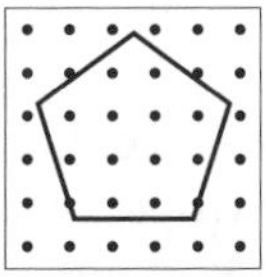

This pentagon has five sides.

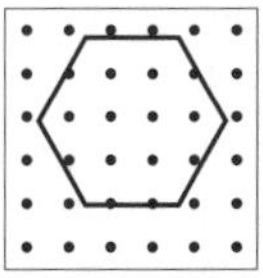

This hexagon has six sides

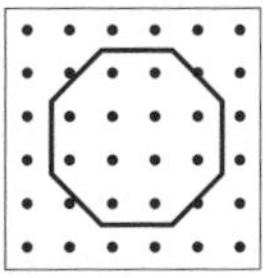

This octagon has eight sides.

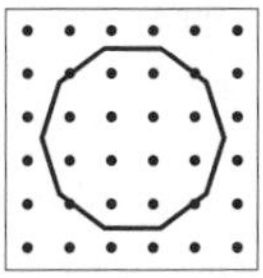

This decagon has ten sides.

Page 10

Hint	Shape Name	Draw the Shape
Example: I have four sides. Two are parallel, and two are not parallel.	trapezoid	
1. All four of my sides are equal.	square	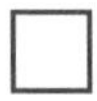
2. My opposite sides are equal and parallel. I have four right angles. I am not a square.	rectangle	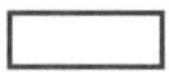
3. I am a polygon with six sides and six angles.	hexagon	
4. I have two perpendicular lines, with three angles.	triangle	
5. I have two pairs of perpendicular lines, two right angles, and five sides.	pentagon	

Page 11
Possible answers include:
1. parallelogram, rhombus
2. square, rectangle
3. parallelogram
4. rhombus, trapezoid
5. square 6. rectangle

Page 12
1. 2 triangles
2. 3 triangles
3. 6 triangles
4. parallelogram and triangle OR three triangles
5. 2 trapezoids OR 1 trapezoid and three triangles OR 1 trapezoid, 1 triangle, and 1 parallelogram OR 2 parallelograms and 2 triangles OR 6 triangles
6. 2 trapezoids OR 1 trapezoid and three triangles OR 1 trapezoid, 1 triangle, and 1 parallelogram OR 2 parallelograms and 2 triangles OR 6 triangles

Page 13
1. octagon 2. triangle
3. diamond 4. circle
5. triangle 6. rectangle
7. trapezoid

Page 14
1. 48 cm 2. 44 in. 3. 57 ft. 4. 64 cm
5. 18 ft. 6. 34 in. 7. 34 cm

Page 15
1. 30 in. 2. 24 in. 3. 36 in.
4. 10 in. 5. 16 in.

Page 16
1. 20 units 2. 18 units 3. 22 units
4. 24 units 5. 30 units 6. 40 units

Page 17
1. 74 ft. 2. 78 in. 3. 808 ft.
4. 54 ft. 5. 128 in.

Page 18
Flowers

Page 19
1. 98 in. 2. 64 cm 3. 40 in.
4. 49 ft. 5. 18 in. 6. 3 in.

Page 20
1. 6 square units 2. 6 square units
3. 7 square units 4. 8 square units
5. 7 square units 6. 8 square units

Page 21
1. 64 sq. ft. 2. 196 sq. ft. 3. 225 sq. ft.
4. 48 sq. ft. 5. 64 sq. ft. 6. 98 sq. ft.
7. living room 8. dining room

Page 22
Hawaii

Answer Pages

Page 23

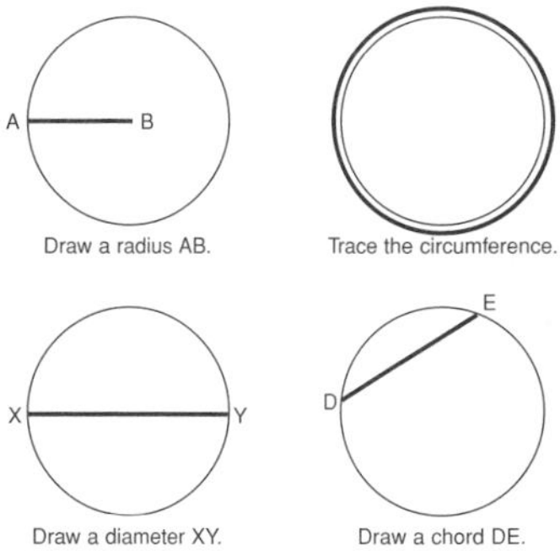

Page 24

1. radius   2. chord   3. radius
4. diameter   5. Y   6. A,B or X,Z

Page 25

1. D   2. AD, DC, BD   3. AC
4. Answers may vary. A red chord drawn through the center of the circle.
5. Answers may vary. Two blue line segments with one endpoint at the center and the other endpoint on the circle.

Page 26

1. 12 in. 2. 27 yd. 3. 36 mm 4. 24 ft.

Page 27

1. 12 mm   2. 14 cm   3. 8 mm
4. 2 ft.   5. 6 yd.

Page 28

1. 2 or more lines of symmetry
2. 1 line of symmetry
3. no line of symmetry
4. 2 or more lines of symmetry
5. 1 line of symmetry
6. no line of symmetry

Page 29

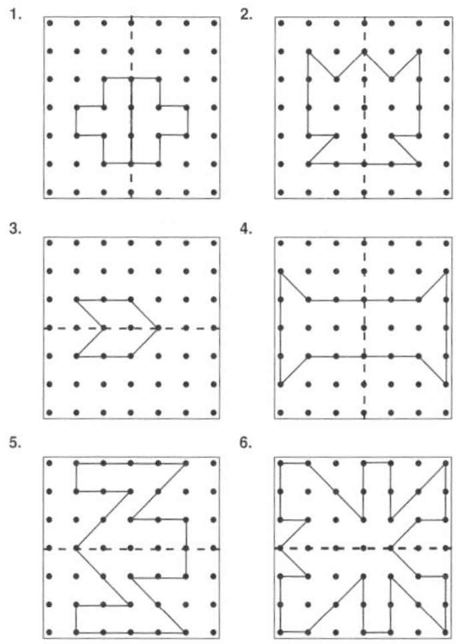

Page 30

1, 4, 5, 6 are correct lines of symmetry and should be colored. 7, 8, 9, should demonstrate any shape or design with a correct line of symmetry.

Page 31

1. slide   2. flip   3. turn
4. slide   5. turn   6. flip

Page 32

1. A,C   2. A,B   3. A,C
4. A,B   5. B,C   6. B,C

Page 33

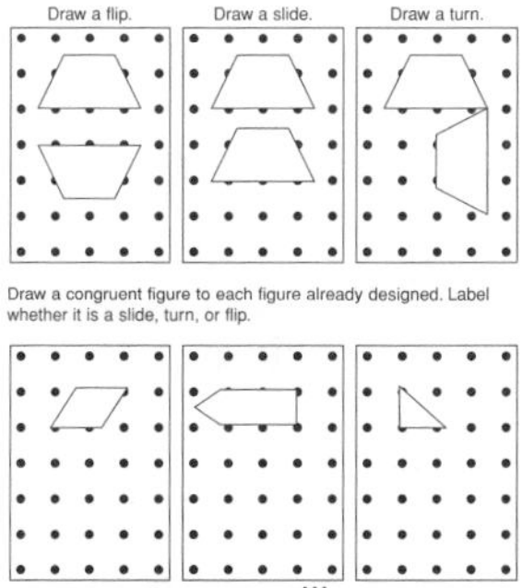

answers will vary

Page 34
1. similar 2. congruent 3. similar
4. congruent
5. image should be identical; the same size and shape
6. image should look similar, can be smaller, larger, or differ in width.

Page 35
1. slide 2. turn 3. flip 4. slide
5. turn 6. flip 7. flip 8. slide

Page 36
1. 8 c.u. 2. 10 c.u. 3. 12 c.u.
4. 14 c.u. 5. 17 c.u. 6. 20 c.u.

Page 37
1. 4 c.u. 2. 6 c.u. 3. 16 c.u.
4. 24 c.u. 5. 30 c.u. 6. 45 c.u.

Page 38
1. 60 cubic mm 2. 24 cubic ft.
3. 210 cubic yd. 4. 432 cubic cm

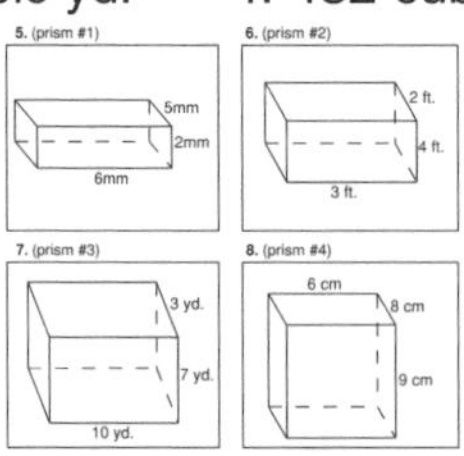

Page 39
1. 16 2. 18 3. 64
4. 40 5. 12 6. 16

Page 40
1. 15,552 cubic in. 2. 72 cubic ft.
3. 90 cubic yd.
4. No, the new stove will not fit because it measures 12,960 cubic in.

Page 41
1. right 2. obtuse 3. acute
4. obtuse 5. acute 6. right
7. acute 8. obtuse 9. right

Page 42
1. acute 2. obtuse 3. right
4. obtuse, acute 5. right, acute
6. right

Page 43
1. acute 2. right 3. right
4. obtuse 5. acute 6. acute

Page 44
1. acute 2. obtuse 3. right
4. obtuse 5. acute 6. right

Page 45
1. B, C
2. 1, 2, 3, 4, 6, 7, 8, 9, 10, 11 (any four)
3. 1, 2; 3, 4; 6, 7; 8, 9; 10, 11
4. AB, AC 5. acute 6. acute
7. acute 8. B or C 9. right

Page 46
1. angle ABC; angle CBA
2. BC, BA 3. B 4. obtuse
5. angle B 6. vertex

Page 47

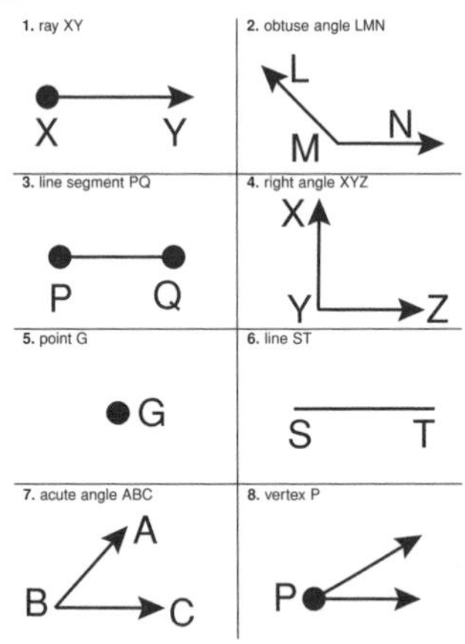

Page 48
1. isosceles 2. scalene 3. equilateral
4. scalene 5. scalene 6. equilateral
7. isosceles 8. isosceles

Answer Pages

Page 49
1. equilateral 2. scalene 3. scalene
4. isosceles 5. equilateral 6. isosceles 7. isosceles 8. scalene

Page 50

Figure	Name	Number of Faces	Number of Edges	Number of Vertices
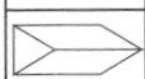	Triangular Prism	5	9	6
	Triangular Pyramid	4	6	4
	Square Pyramid	5	8	5

1. triangular prism
2. square pyramid
3. triangular pyramid
4. triangular prism
5. triangular pyramid
6. square pyramid
7. triangular prism/square pyramid
8. triangular pyramid

Page 51
1. 48° 2. 45° 3. 15° 4. 60°

Page 52
1. scalene or isosceles 2. isosceles
3. scalene
4. equilateral, scalene, or isosceles
5. equilateral
6. scalene or isosceles
7. right

Page 53
1. 8 2. 3 3. 7 4. 1 5. 4 6. 6

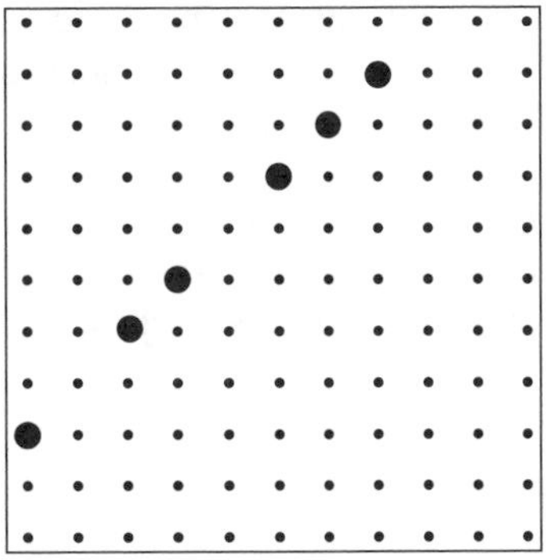

Page 54
1. grapes 2. sugar
3. milk 4. eggs
5. yogurt 6. apples
7. ketchup 8. ham
9. strawberry jelly 10. cheese

Page 55

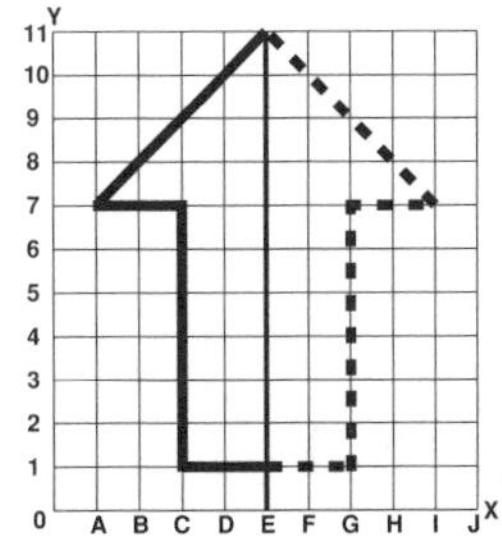

Page 56
1. (5, 1) 2. (3, 1) 3. (6, 4)
4. (1, 3) 5. (2, 5) 6. (4, 6)

Page 57
Parallel Lines: hexagon, parallelogram, octagon
Perpendicular Lines: right triangle
Both: pentagon, rectangle, square

Page 58
1. regular 2. not regular
3. not regular 4. regular
5. not regular 6. regular
7. not regular 8. regular
9. regular 10. not regular
11. not regular 12. regular
13. All shapes have sides that are equal lengths and have equal angles.
14. All sides and angles are not the same size.

Page 59
With: 1, 3, 4, 6
Without: 2, 5, 7

8. All are regular polygons.
9. All are not regular polygons.

Page 60
All equilateral triangles have three acute angles.

Page 61

1. windmill and store
2. (5,3)
3. (7,1), bus stop, (7,7)
4. (3,4)
5. mail box
6. (7,7) and (5,7)

Page 62
Death Valley

Page 63

Draw an ice cream cone using 1 triangle and 3 circles.	
Draw a train using 1 triangle, 1 rectangle, and 3 circles	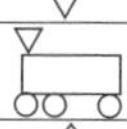
Draw a house using 1 pentagon, 1 rectangle, 2 squares, and 1 circle.	
Draw a robot using 1 octagon, 3 ovals, 4 rectangles, and 1 square.	answers will vary
Draw flowers in a pot using 1 trapezoid, 3 rectangles, 3 hexagons, and 18 ovals.	

Page 64

1. Triangles cannot have two right angles. Right triangles are the only triangles that have a right angle. A right triangle has only one right angle.
2. Their circles are the same size because the radius is half of the diameter.
3. All angles of an octagon are obtuse.

Page 65

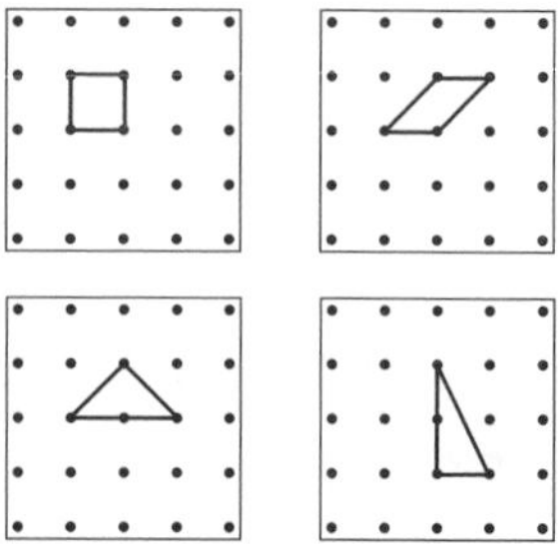

Page 66

s	l	h	j	r	x	x	q	y	h	d	q	w	c
n	i	u	e	e	n	d	o	t	r	o	u	x	t
o	o	l	l	c	o	n	g	s	b	p	a	t	o
g	s	r	g	t	g	o	b	q	s	j	d	j	z
a	e	q	n	a	y	g	y	u	u	c	r	f	m
x	c	c	a	n	l	a	q	a	w	x	i	y	w
e	v	f	i	g	o	t	g	r	a	g	l	u	f
h	f	f	r	l	p	n	c	e	i	f	a	w	e
h	h	g	t	e	g	e	r	o	n	v	t	r	z
i	x	e	m	a	c	p	n	h	l	m	e	b	k
z	r	t	r	a	p	e	z	o	i	d	r	l	x
a	z	z	y	f	v	m	v	h	f	u	a	w	h
z	k	d	p	k	t	c	t	h	w	i	l	t	i
l	p	q	e	v	i	n	h	y	z	v	s	v	j

Page 67

1. cylinder
2. rectangular prism
3. cube
4. sphere
5. cone
6. Answers will vary. They may include the following: The figure is a square pyramid. It has 5 vertices, 8 edges, and 5 faces.
7. Side A shapes are quadrilaterals. They are all closed shapes.
8. Side B shapes are not regular polygons. They are open figures and do not have parallel and congruent sides or angles.

Page 68

Page 69

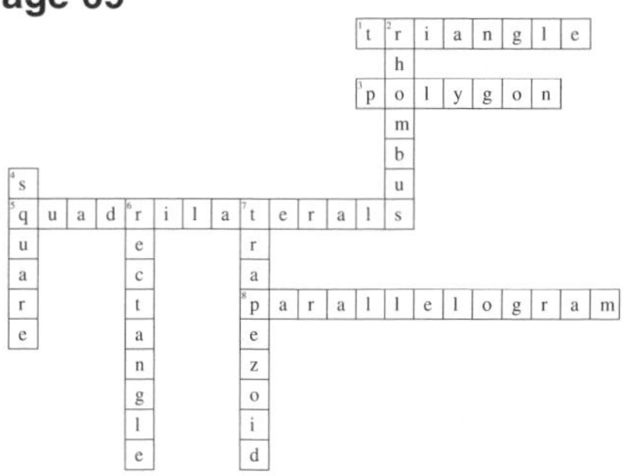

Page 70

1. 1, 2, 3, 5, 6, 8, 9
2. 4, 7 because they have no sides or corners
3. tangram

Notes

Five things I'm thankful for:

1. ____________________
2. ____________________
3. ____________________
4. ____________________
5. ____________________